NEW TESTAMENT CHRISTIANITY IN THE

ROMAN WORLD

"A collection of collections"

CANON - list of writings developed over time comprised of the OT & NT

Prior texts referred to context of teachings on Jesus Christ

SCRIPTURE - any text "divinely inspired" therefore authoritative - did not end with 1st & 2nd generation Christians - but an on-going, continuing reality.

ESSENTIALS OF BIBLICAL STUDIES

Series Editor
Patricia K. Tull, Louisville Presbyterian Theological Seminary

READING HEBREW BIBLE NARRATIVES
John A. Dearman

THE HISTORY OF BRONZE AND IRON AGE ISRAEL
Victor H. Matthews

NEW TESTAMENT CHRISTIANITY IN THE ROMAN WORLD
Harry O. Maier

WOMEN IN THE NEW TESTAMENT WORLD
Susan E. Hylen

NEW TESTAMENT CHRISTIANITY IN THE ROMAN WORLD

HARRY O. MAIER

OXFORD
UNIVERSITY PRESS

OXFORD
UNIVERSITY PRESS

Oxford University Press is a department of the University of Oxford. It furthers
the University's objective of excellence in research, scholarship, and education
by publishing worldwide. Oxford is a registered trade mark of Oxford University
Press in the UK and certain other countries.

Published in the United States of America by Oxford University Press
198 Madison Avenue, New York, NY 10016, United States of America.

© Oxford University Press 2019

Library of Congress Cataloging-in-Publication Data
Names: Maier, Harry O., 1959– author.
Title: New Testament Christianity in the Roman world / Harry O. Maier.
Description: New York, NY : Oxford University Press, [2018] |
Includes ibliographical references and index.
Identifiers: LCCN 2018016585 (print) | LCCN 2018038029 (ebook) |
ISBN 9780190264413 (updf) | ISBN 9780190264420 (epub) |
ISBN 9780190264437 (online content) | ISBN 9780190264390 |
ISBN 9780190264390 (cloth) | ISBN 9780190264406 (paperback)
Subjects: LCSH: Bible. New Testament—History of contemporary events. |
Church history—Primitive and early church, ca. 30–600.
Classification: LCC BS2410 (ebook) | LCC BS2410 .M334 2018 (print) |
DDC 270.1—dc23
LC record available at https://lccn.loc.gov/2018016585

9 8 7 6 5 4 3 2 1

Paperback printed by Sheridan Books, Inc., United States of America
Hardback printed by Bridgeport National Bindery, Inc., United States of America

For my students

CONTENTS

FIGURES

TABLES

ACKNOWLEDGMENTS

I am grateful for the assistance of a number of people in the production of this study. Clifford Ando, Jan Bremmer, and Jörg Rüpke patiently answered many questions regarding ancient data. I also benefited from the expertise of Esther Eidenow, Kristine Iara, and Georgia Petridou. The editorial assistance and advice of Richard Gordon were invaluable. He read earlier drafts of chapters and saved me from numerous errors of fact and interpretation. Maryann Amor, Philip Francis, and Philip Harrison proofread earlier drafts and offered insightful comments, without which there would have been significantly more stylistic infelicities and inconsistencies than those that have survived their close scrutiny. Elizabeth Christensen and June Pearson, nonacademics, helped me to keep the discussion accessible to nonspecialists. My colleagues Jason Byassee and Nicola Hayward, as well as former students James Magee, Trevor Malkinson, and Rhian Walker, provided valuable feedback on different chapters. I am grateful to the Max Weber Centre for Advanced Cultural and Social Studies at the University of Erfurt for its hospitality and the interdisciplinary conversations of its Fellows and guests that helped me to form many of the ideas and the general approach developed here. Jörg Rüpke was a most gracious host and interlocutor. Finally, I am thankful for the generous funding of the Alexander von Humboldt Foundation and the German Academic Exchange Service that enabled me to complete this book.

SERIES INTRODUCTION

The past three decades have seen an explosion of approaches to study of the Bible, as older exegetical methods have been joined by a variety of literary, anthropological, and social models. Interfaith collaboration has helped change the field, and the advent of more cultural diversity among biblical scholars in the West and around the world has broadened our reading and interpretation of the Bible. These changes have also fueled interest in Scripture's past, including both the ancient Near Eastern and Mediterranean worlds out of which Scripture came and the millennia of premodern interpretation through which it traveled to our day. The explosion of information and perspectives is so vast that no one textbook can any longer address the many needs of seminaries and colleges where the Bible is studied.

In addition to these developments in the field itself are changes in the field's students. Traditionally the domain of seminaries, graduate schools, and college and university religion classes, biblical study now also takes place in a host of alternative venues. As lay leadership in local churches develops, nontraditional, weekend, and online preparatory classes have mushroomed. As seminaries in Africa, Asia, and Latin America have grown, the particular need for inexpensive and easily available materials has become clear. As religious controversies over the Bible's origins and norms continue to dominate the airwaves, congregation members and even curious nonreligious folk seek reliable paths into particular topics. And teachers themselves continue to seek guidance in areas of the ever-expanding field of scriptural study with which they may be less than familiar.

A third wave of changes also makes this series timely: shifts in the publishing industry itself. Technologies and knowledge are shifting so rapidly that large books are out of date almost before they are in print. The Internet and the growing popularity of e-books call for flexibility and accessibility in marketing and sales. If the days when one expert can sum up the field in a textbook are gone, also gone are the days when large, expensive multi-authored tomes are attractive to students, teachers, and other readers.

During my own years of seminary teaching, I have tried to find just the right book or books for just the right price, and at just the right reading level for my students, with just enough information to orient them without drowning them in excess reading. For all these reasons, this search was all too often less than successful. So I was excited to be asked to help Oxford University Press assemble a select crew of leading scholars to create a series that would respond to such classroom challenges. Essentials of Biblical Studies comprises freestanding, relatively brief, accessibly written books that provide an orientation to the Bible's contents, its ancient contexts, its interpretive methods and history, and its themes and figures. Rather than a one-size-had-better-fit-all approach, these books may be mixed and matched to suit the objectives of a variety of classroom venues, as well as the needs of individuals wishing to find their way into unfamiliar topics.

I am confident that our authors will join me in returning enthusiastic thanks to the editorial staff at Oxford University Press for their support and guidance, especially Theo Calderara, who shepherded the project in its early days, and Dr. Steve Wiggins, who has been a most wise and steady partner in this work since joining OUP in 2013.

Patricia K. Tull
Series Editor

NEW TESTAMENT CHRISTIANITY IN THE

ROMAN WORLD

Map of the Roman Empire, mid-first century CE. From Bart Ehrman
The New Testament, 6th edition, Oxford University Press.

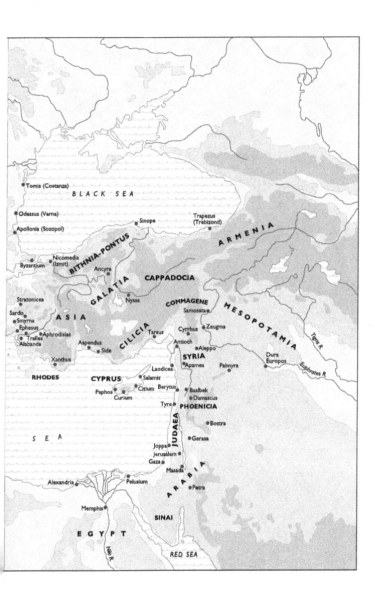

INTRODUCTION

For Christians are not distinguished from the rest of humanity by country, language, or custom. For nowhere do they live in cities of their own, nor do they speak some unusual dialect, nor do they practice an eccentric way of life. . . . But while they live in both Greek and barbarian cities, as each one's lot was cast, and follow the local customs in dress and food and other aspects of life, at the same time they demonstrate the remarkable and admittedly unusual character of their own citizenship. They live in their own countries, but only as nonresidents; they participate in everything as citizens, and endure everything as foreigners. Every foreign country is their fatherland, and every fatherland is foreign. They marry like everyone else, and have children, but they do not expose their offspring. They share their food but not their wives. They are in the flesh, but they do not live according to the flesh. They live on earth, but their citizenship is in heaven.

—*Epistle to Diognetus* 5.1–9[1]

MAKING THE FAMILIAR STRANGE

This book is an introduction to the Roman world of the eastern Mediterranean and its intersections with the New Testament writings that follow the Gospels, as well as other Christian and Jewish literature contemporary with them.[2] Under five broad headings of religion, empire, city, household, and self, its chief aim is to orient readers to overarching social phenomena that constituted the Roman world and invite them to consider ways in which each aspect presents important contexts for understanding the contents of the New Testament and the emergence of Christianity.

An awareness of these contexts is essential to biblical study for at least two reasons. First, as the above quotation from the second-century *Epistle to Diognetus* suggests, it reminds us that Christianity did not fall perfectly formed out of heaven, but was practiced and developed under particular historical and social conditions. The *Epistle* is an anonymous apology addressed to an otherwise unknown Diognetus, whom the writer seeks to win over to the Christian faith. The passage is of particular value because it reveals a faith lived amid the daily structures of society (here, city and family). Christians do not talk or dress differently from their neighbors, the author writes, but rather share with them the cultural and material aspects of daily life, where they also express their distinctiveness through the pursuit of a particular set of virtues. The writer argues that it is in engagement *with*, not isolation *from*, the conditions of daily life that Christian faith reveals itself. However, the corollary of a faith that lives in the world is that the world shapes the faith that is lived. He thus draws on the language of politics ("citizenship," "fatherland") to portray a countercultural identity of belonging to a heavenly city. Christians and non-Christians inhabit a shared environment and a set of values that go along with them. Indeed, the success of the apologist's argument depends on a recognition of those shared goods. His chief point in the above quotation is that Christians live their earthly citizenship better than non-Christians do because they follow a higher ethical standard.

A study that attends to the lived realities of the ancient world helps to put flesh and blood into texts that can otherwise be read as disembodied—as religious teachings existing outside the constraints of time and context—rather than writings whose aim was to help audiences apply their beliefs to daily life and negotiate conflicts over interpretation and religious practice.

Here we have the second reason why awareness of context is essential. When we recognize how ancient context determined what was written, we realize that our contemporary context determines how we read it. Understanding this helps us to gain a better understanding of ourselves. As the following discussion unfolds, we will discover that the phenomena it addresses are strangely familiar. Contemporary ideas about religion, empire (for current relevance, consider that we are living with the decline of the British Empire, the collapse of the Soviet Union, and the domination of an American economic imperium), city, family, and self share a long genealogy that stretches back to the first two centuries of the Common Era, the period this book discusses, and beyond that to classical antiquity and the ancient Near East. When we engage them, we are in an important sense studying ourselves, because their modern expressions often bear the genetic trace of their origins in sometimes obvious, but usually invisible, ways.

Family resemblance presents both an opportunity and a risk. The opportunity is to discover the ways that many contemporary notions have developed out of ancient ones, and thereby recognize ways in which the past has shaped the modern world. At the same time, their apparent familiarity carries the risk of imposing modern understandings upon ancient phenomena that, while sharing a similar vocabulary (for example, the Latin cognates *religio, imperium, civitas, familia*), were understood and practiced in ways strikingly different from contemporary ones.

The risk becomes greater in the study of the New Testament because, in addition to the fact that the Bible's texts are historical documents steeped in the worlds of their origins, they are also religious ones to which billions of people turn for guidance. Without recognition of the ancient social worlds in which the

New Testament's writings were composed, there is a danger of being misled by modern ideas imported into biblical passages and then returned as divinely willed religious ones, or by tearing texts out of their contexts and simplistically imposing them on modern situations and debates. Beliefs in a seven-day creation and a young earth, as well as debates over homosexuality, abortion, divorce, and the ordination of women, are timely examples of the way the Bible is used anachronistically to challenge or endorse modern ideas. We can see that the stakes are high when we read biblical authors forbidding women to have authority over men, instructing them to remain silent in church, exhorting them to gain their salvation by bearing children (1 Tim. 2:11–15), telling slaves to obey their masters (Col. 3:11; Eph. 6:5–8; 1 Pet. 2:18–25), and forecasting the end of history in a final apocalyptic battle (Rev. 20:7–9), followed by the ultimate in global warming when the earth and all the works of humankind will be consumed by fire (2 Pet. 3:10–12). All through history people have read such passages without reference to social and historical context, often with disastrous results for women, minorities, the vulnerable, the global order, and the environment. Such a history makes the study of the New Testament against the backdrop of its larger Roman world not only necessary but also urgent.

In short, this book aims to make the familiar strange by locating the New Testament and its audiences in a variety of overlapping but distinct ancient contexts. In doing so, it seeks to describe the dynamic and complex social contexts in which earliest Christianity developed and was practiced.

"THE" NEW TESTAMENT

As the title of this book indicates, the focus of this discussion is on the ways in which the Roman world furnished a context for beliefs and practices found in the New Testament and other early Christian literature. It is worth noting that use of the singular definite article to describe *the* New Testament can be misleading. While it is a single volume, its contents are described in the plural: "the *books* of the New Testament." The diversity of the Christian canon is too easily erased by reference to it as a single entity, which often leads to cross-referencing without attention to the differing literary and historical contexts of selected passages. Even the phrase "the books of the New Testament" can distort their contents, as it may lead to the mistaken perception that because it is made up of "books," each one must be similar in form. In fact, a diversity of texts in both form and content (Gospels, history, letters, sermons, hymns, speeches, apocalypses, and so on) constitute the body of literature the New Testament represents. It was written over several decades by authors who did not know each other and were usually unaware of each other's writings. We might think of the various New Testament writings as a set of historical snapshots taken by different people at different times, places, and situations that eventually found their way through a long process of accumulation and arrangement into a single volume. These snapshots form more of a collage of images than a single picture or self-consistent whole, even as their presence alongside one another has led to reinterpretations of single writings through reference to the others, including those of the Jewish Bible.

To add to this complex picture, within each single New Testament writing there is often evidence of additions to and subtractions from the text, or of the forging together of originally separate texts into one writing (as in the case, for example, of 2 Corinthians, which many scholars argue comprises two separate letter fragments, and some contend is made up of as many as six). John's Revelation and the Book of Acts show a large variety of manuscript traditions and variations. Further, in the case of the Synoptic Gospels (Matthew, Mark, and Luke), there was direct word-for-word copying, rearrangement by Matthew and Luke of the order of a preexisting narrative most scholars believe originated with Mark, interpolation of new contents, and rewriting as well as omission of received ones. Notwithstanding the stern warning in Revelation of punishment to anyone who changes a word of its text (Rev. 22:18–19), the manuscript tradition of the Apocalypse shows many scribes doing just that, even as hundreds of others were doing the same with the rest of the Christian canon. The fact that the various writings of the New Testament were subject to editing through (sometimes dramatic) alteration of received tradition as well as interpolation (for example, the longer endings of Mark [16:9–20]; the story of the woman caught in adultery [John 8:3–11], and possibly John 21) indicates that they were formed in living communities that sought to make their content as relevant as possible to the situations of their audiences, and to serve particular interests. Unlike today, where mass printing, international teams of expert scholars, and chapter and verse create a largely stable and unchanging New Testament text, ancient scribes had a very different relationship to the literary tradition they received.

This also makes the idea of authorship much more complicated than one might expect. It is customary to state that Matthew wrote his Gospel for one community, Mark for another, Luke for a third, and John for a fourth. It is true that we can adduce certain features characteristic of each Gospel that allow us to hypothesize general and sometimes specific historical backdrops for each writing. However, once we see that these texts have complicated histories of transmission, as well as the probability of attribution of a single name to each at a later date, any singular idea of an author or simplistic notion of a community of addressees becomes problematic. Is the author of Mark an original author, a single later editor, or its last editor? Is a Book of Revelation with its manifold textual variants one Book of Revelation or many? Many scholars agree that 2 Corinthians consists of two or more separate letter fragments composed by Paul and collated by a later editor. What, then, does it means to speak of "the author" of 2 Corinthians? Was it Paul or a later writer? The New Testament is witness to a dynamic lived religion that emerged and gradually coalesced within a particular set of historical conditions. Over time, the early church told a certain story about these texts that in part served a polemical aim of limiting the diversity of an emerging religious tradition by championing one set of interpretations and one story of their origins over others. Eusebius of Caesarea (263–339 CE), for example, in his fourth-century *Ecclesiastical History*, defended a New Testament restricted to four Gospels by defending their apostolic pedigree: Matthew and John were disciples of Jesus and wrote their Gospels as memoirs, while Mark constructed his writing from Peter's preaching, and Luke based his on records from eyewitnesses.[3] Whereas the early church sought uniformity and consistency in the story of the emergence of the canon, the material evidence of the New Testament points to a much more complicated reality of copying, editing, interpolation, and correction in often polemical contexts. When we speak of the New Testament and its books, we must resist the temptation to think of a single author or single set of writers composing a set of stable texts with a single set of intentions. Words like "New Testament," "books," "Matthew," "Mark," "Luke," "John," "Paul," and "Revelation" are shorthand for much more complicated historical phenomena.

THE NEW TESTAMENT CANON

The formation of the canon remains a topic of scholarly debate. The twenty-seven writings that came to constitute the New Testament represent the barest fraction of first- and second-century literature associated with emerging Christian tradition. Further, they are textual artifacts of a religion that included many other things alongside writing and reading/listening, among which were worship, prayer, eating, practices of hospitality, rituals of baptism, healing, exorcism, and so on. These texts record a small fraction of early Christian belief and practice as seen from the particular points of view of their authors. Nevertheless, they represent a chief means we have to understand the various characteristics of the religion they represent. It is an important one, since from an early date, Christian belief was communicated by way of texts that were, from the very start, read publically in communal settings (1 Thess. 5:27; Col. 4:16; 1 Tim. 4:13; Acts 15:22–35), and that, by the end of the first or early second century, were being brought together into various collections (see below). Justin Martyr (100–165), writing in the mid-second century, furnishes the earliest record of a public reading at a weekly Eucharistic gathering, where believers congregated to hear "Gospels" and "the memoirs of the apostles or the writings of the prophets."[4] The fact that from an early date such writings took the form of codices (i.e., books), rather than more typical scrolls, suggests a desire to collect different and variously authored writings into a single book for study, cross-referencing, public reading, and proclamation, and it reflects the literary character (what has been called "the textual habit") of the movement.

How did these particular texts, rather than other writings, become part of the Christian Bible? First, we can dispense with a regularly rehearsed and popular conspiracy theory (repeated most recently in Dan Brown's *The Da Vinci Code*), positing that the contents of the New Testament were determined though a heavy-handed political process at a meeting of bishops (usually linked with the Council of Nicaea in 325 CE), who rejected any writing inimical to imperial rule and Christian orthodoxy and only included ones that could be used to legitimate a social religious order supportive of emperors and bishops. Furthermore, the theory goes, they burned any books that did not make the cut and condemned those associated with them as heretics who should be ruthlessly hunted down and murdered. Such ideas may be entertaining, but they are certainly fictional. In the first place, the popular definition of the canon as a closed set of scripture books appeared for the first time only in the 18th century, and is thus a modern notion. As for self-interested church and political officials, it is an odd way to legitimate imperial power and ecclesiastical authority by creating a collection of writings to present the following story: The main character was crucified by Roman authorities. He had berated his disciples for their stupidity and confusion (Mark 8:14–21). They betrayed, denied, and abandoned him. Peter and Paul, the chief founders of his church, were at loggerheads (Gal. 2:11–14). An emperor was cast as a beast installed by Satan (Rev. 13:1–8), and the imperial capital personified as a prostitute who gets drunk on human blood (Rev. 17:1–6).

As for the process of collection, there was no single event or set of people to decide what would or would not be in the canon, and there was no precise date when the canon definitively coalesced into a universally accepted list of books. We should rather think of a slow organic process of formation over a relatively long period. From the fourth century onward (some think earlier), leading Christian authorities composed lists of books they considered canonical that were similar but not identical in content. The evidence points to independent processes of formation and ex post facto recognition rather than a single moment of invention. Finally, it should be stated that the canonical process is still underway. While there is broad consensus about the Bible's contents, there is no single list of canonical texts upon which all Christians around the world agree, especially with reference to the Old Testament and the Apocrypha. Parts of the Nestorian church do not include the

Book of Revelation in its canon. Martin Luther argued the Apocalypse is not divinely inspired, and he demoted the Book of James as an "epistle of straw."

When examining the emergence of the New Testament, it is helpful to distinguish the notion of "scripture" from that of "canon." Modern usage equates "Holy Scripture" with the Bible. While the early church would have agreed that the canon was scripture, it did not restrict scripture to the Bible. In early Christian usage the term "scripture" was a more general word used to describe any text believed to be divinely inspired and hence authoritative. The broad term reflects the early belief that divine and prophetic inspiration did not end with the first two generations of Christians, but was rather a continuing reality. "*Kanōn*," from a Greek word that means "rule" or "measure," describes a more specific phenomenon whose meaning developed over time. Early Christian writers repeatedly cite writings (many of which survive only in fragments) that did not become part of the canon but were for them authoritative sources of divine revelation and instruction for belief and practice. During the fourth century, "canon" came to be associated with a list of writings that defined a specific set of documents comprising the Old and New Testaments. Before this period, "canon" did not refer to a body of texts, but rather to the content of teachings believed to preserve apostolic instruction and proclamation regarding the revelation of God in Jesus of Nazareth, against which any claims to Christian teaching were to be measured. In the later second and the third centuries, a variety of figures such as Irenaeus, the bishop of Lyons (ca. 130–202), the North Africa theologian Tertullian (ca. 160–220), as well as Clement (ca. 150–215) and Origen (ca. 185–254), who were both teachers in Alexandria, all used the Greek and Latin phrases "the canon of truth" (*ho kanōn alētheias/ regula veritatis*) and "the rule of faith" (*ho kanōn tēs pisteōs/ regula fidei*) to describe the criteria for measuring true Christian teaching. In part, they deployed them as a polemical means of refuting a variety of ideas and writings claiming to originate with or preserve Jesus's teachings, as well as new teachings brought about through divine revelations. To a degree, these notions were a response to an explosion of second-century writings that included gospels, letters, apocalypses, apocryphal acts, revelations, and so on. Irenaeus was the first to name Matthew, Mark, Luke, and John as the four definitive Gospels, and he restricted their number to four by arguing that each corresponds to the four directions of the compass, thereby indicating their universality for all humankind (*Against Heresies* 3.11.7–9). It is a forced argument, and it reflects his desire to oppose alleged heretics who relied for their ideas on one or more noncanonical gospels. On the other hand, a variety of other writings that would eventually be excluded from the New Testament, such as the *Gospel of Peter*, the *Epistle of Barnabas*, the *Shepherd of Hermas*, the *Acts of Paul*, and the *Didache*, were widely cited as authoritative. An early harmony of the four Gospels called the *Diatessaron*, created in the middle of the second century by an eastern Christian named Tatian, was treated as scripture and on par with the four Gospels by the Syrian church well into the fifth century.

The first author to use the term *kanōn* expressly to describe a list of biblical writings was Athanasius, the bishop of Alexandria (296–373), in his "Festal Letter" of 367 CE. Earlier in the fourth century, Eusebius of Caesarea used the word "catalogue" (*katalogos*) to describe a set of writings as "recognized" (*homologoumena*), in distinction to three other classes of texts that he called "disputed" (*antilegomena*), "spurious" (*notha*), and "heretical." Among the disputed texts he named James, Jude, 2 Peter, 2 and 3 John, Hebrews, and the *Shepherd of Hermas* (in another passage listed with the *Acts of Paul* and the *Apocalypse of Peter* as spurious).[5] His categorization centered on a notion of broad consensus rather than a fixed list of writings. Eusebius identified four criteria for including books in the "recognized list": apostolicity, orthodoxy, antiquity, and universality or wide use. The fact that he developed such a set of criteria to adjudicate the status of writings in use indicates he knew of the existence of other New Testament collections that were largely similar to but also different from one another. Some writings, for example, were revered in particular localities for a variety of reasons, some of them survived purely by chance and others were not known or used in other places. A few (such as the Book of Hebrews) were accepted by some churches and rejected elsewhere.

In 331 CE, the emperor Constantine commissioned Eusebius to produce fifty Bibles for use in the many churches of the empire's new capital, Constantinople. Some suggest this was an important catalyst for fourth-century canonical formation more generally. The oldest known manuscripts of the entire Christian Bible (i.e., the Old and New Testaments) are codices from the fourth century: the Codex Sinaiticus (named after St. Catherine's Monastery at Mount Sinai, where it was discovered in the 19th century) and Codex Vaticanus (named after its location in the Vatican Library; see Figure 1.1). It is perhaps significant that they are contemporary with the canonical lists of Eusebius and Athanasius. Some argue that their existence is testament to a conceptual transition from scripture to canon underway in the fourth century.

While Eusebius and Athanasius point to a later date for the formulation of a canonical list of sacred texts, another text, the *Muratorian Fragment*, has been used to argue that the canon was largely settled at a much earlier date. The *Fragment* is an eighty-five-line text named after Ludovico Antonio Muratori (1672–1750), who discovered it in a seventh-century codex. It is a Latin translation of a Greek writing that claims to have been written in 170 CE and comprises a list of books of the New Testament that includes the Wisdom of Solomon and the *Apocalypse of Peter*, but does not mention Hebrews, 1 and 2

FIGURE 1.1 A leaf from P[46] of 2 Corinthians 13:5–13 (P.Mich.inv. 6238), 200–250 CE. Image digitally reproduced with the permission of the Papyrology Collection, Graduate Library, University of Michigan (www.lib.umich.edu/papyrology-collection).

Peter, 3 John, or James. If its date is accepted, it is the oldest extant list of New Testament writings and could be evidence of a stable canon, as well as the movement from scripture to canon, well before the fourth century. There is continuing debate, however, concerning its date, and there are compelling reasons to believe it comes from the fourth century and reflects processes of canonization of that later period.

Whatever view one finally accepts concerning the date of a relatively stable canon, it is important to note that a largely settled New Testament is not equivalent to a universally shared Greek text of its contents. There are no surviving original biblical texts—none—so modern critical editions of the Greek New Testament present an approximation of the earliest version of writings determined by analysis of manuscript variations by teams of experts. Differences are listed at the bottom of each page of the text and testify to a text that was copied and used in varieties of circumstances and contexts. In other words, manuscript variations reveal a New Testament with a complicated genesis, but more importantly they represent a lived, organic religion.

A COLLECTION OF COLLECTIONS

Whatever side of the argument one takes with respect to canonical formation, there is evidence that well before the fourth century, collections of texts were forming and circulating independently of one another. Generally, scholars identify three bodies of literature that formed separate collections: the four Gospels, the letters of Paul, and the general or catholic Epistles (James, 1–2 Peter, 1–3 John, and Jude). Acts, Hebrews, and Revelation represent idiosyncratic evidence. This again points to a slow process of accretion and circulation. The canon is a collection of collections.

We have already mentioned Irenaeus's reference to the four Gospels, which indicates that by the last decades of the second century a version of them was treated as a self-contained group. A papyrus from ca. 250 CE (P^{45}) is the oldest material representative of the four-Gospel collection and is, significantly, in the form of a codex (i.e., a book rather than separate papyrus leaves or a scroll), thus probably indicating that they were being read in the light of one another. Scholars continue to debate when names became affixed to these writings. Some argue that this happened at a very early date, while others contend that the Gospels were first anonymous and became attached to apostolic names only later as a means of asserting their authority over other writings, such as the *Gospel of Thomas* and the *Gospel of Mary*, which were discovered in 1945 at Nag Hammadi in Egypt, together with numerous other codices that shed important light on early Christianity. The *Gospel of Mary* can arguably be dated to the mid-second century, and the *Gospel of Thomas* is perhaps as old as Mark.

The development of the thirteen-letter Pauline corpus has provided researchers with many happy hours of study. A collection of ten letters, arranged in order of length, and excluding 1–2 Timothy and Titus, was in circulation during the first half of the second century. Marcion of Sinope (ca. 85–160 CE) promoted a collection of the same ten letters together with an edited version of Luke's Gospel as the revelation of the true God whom Jesus had come to proclaim. He rejected the other Gospels and the whole of the Hebrew Bible as inspired by an inferior deity. In the twentieth century, there was a scholarly consensus that Marcion was the first to create a New Testament canon, which was the catalyst for the church to create a counter-canon to oppose him and other heretics. However, the evidence shows that Marcion revised a preexisting Pauline corpus of letters arranged from longest to shortest, grouped together as epistles to seven churches (parallel with the seven messages to the seven churches in Rev. 2–3). Textual comparison of Marcion's text with other Pauline fragments suggests that the collection Marcion revised was already in existence by 100 CE. A papyrus from 200 CE (P^{46}—see Figure 1.2) is the oldest material representative of the Pauline corpus (again without 1–2 Timothy and Titus, but the manuscript is incomplete). Like the earlier collection, it arranges the letters from longest to shortest, but with Romans followed by Hebrews (suggesting a Pauline attribution). P^{46} is a codex and indicates, as does P^{45}, circulation as a collection.

The third collection, the seven general or catholic Epistles, does not receive treatment as a group until the fourth century, when Eusebius's *Church History* (2.23.25) identifies them as "disputed" (2.25.3). These letters were cited relatively infrequently by church writers of the second and third centuries, and probably were not gathered into a corpus until ca. 300 CE.

Luke The first clear citation of Acts is by Irenaeus at the end of the second century, after which time the book is quoted frequently. Hebrews appears in P^{46}, a manuscript of the Greek East, but because of its rigorist teaching that rejected a second repentance for post-baptismal sin, it ran counter to the penitential theology of the West and was not accepted there until the mid-fourth century. The Book of Revelation was widely quoted in the West throughout the second century, but its eschatology resulted in it not being accepted in the East until the late fourth century, and in other churches reluctantly many centuries later.

Having sketched in some detail the processes of canonical formation, it is important to return to the *Epistle to Diognetus* cited above. The New Testament is obviously central to the way Christianity defines itself. However, the canonical processes just outlined point to a dynamic and lived religious reality, spread across vast distances, and with different interests and commitments from region to region and from one period to the next. The New Testament testifies to entangled realities of religious

FIGURE 1.2 Codex Vaticanus, 2 Thessalonians 3:11–18 and Hebrews 1:1–2:4, fourth century CE. From Wikimediacommons (Commons.wikimedia.org/wiki/File:Codex_Vaticanus_B,_2Thess._3,11-18,_Hebr._1,1-2,2.jpg#/media/File:Codex_Vaticanus_B,_2Thess._3,11-18,_Hebr._1,1-2,2.jpg).

commitments and daily life. One of the reasons for the survival of a writing that would eventually become part of a defined body of sacred texts and its dispersion around the Roman Empire was that it was perceived to be relevant to everyday life. A number of other issues played into survival as well, among which we can include politics, gender, and economics, to name only a few. Writings that promoted support of the state and traditional family structures were more likely to have universal appeal than those that called for rejection of them. However, a number of writings that *did* call such things into question were also useful and appealing and found universal adoption. New Testament writings reflect a host of intriguing and historically messy stories. In other words, early Christianity was not a book or even a church; it was individuals and communities living in space and time. Like the formation of the canon, this makes early Christianity a complex phenomenon incapable of being described or understood through appeal to any single theory of origins or historical narrative.

This brings us to a phrase in the title of this book, "New Testament Christianity." It is meant to describe a general set of phenomena taking in place in communities represented by biblical writings, but it is important that readers are not misled by it into thinking that Christianity was one thing that true believers held in common in a geographically dispersed movement. The New Testament attests to a diversity of ways of believing and living associated with the teachings and person of Jesus of Nazareth and reports fierce divisions over what being a follower of Jesus should entail. In a memorable passage Paul describes Christians undermining his mission "false apostles, deceitful workers, disguising themselves as apostles of Christ" (2 Cor. 11:13). The author of 1 John condemns a group of believers who reject the physical incarnation of Jesus as anti-Christ (1 John 2:18–25). Jude 4 pillories "certain intruders [who have] stolen in among you . . . who pervert the grace of our God into licentiousness and deny our only Master and Lord, Jesus Christ." We can expect that if the people Paul, John, and Jude pillory were able to present their teachings to us, they would tell a different story. Passages such as these suggest that we should not imagine a single Christianity in the period we are discussing, with a universally agreed upon creed and set of ethical commitments. Rather we should think of a shifting and dynamic set of beliefs and practices that were specific to differing lived contexts and that were often in competition with one another. We should imagine that beliefs and behavioral norms that were salient in one social situation could be different in another one. Already in the second century Christians started to tell a story about Christianity as a single united thing passed on in an uninterrupted chain of instruction from the apostles onward, corrupted by heretics whom Satan sent in order to destroy a pristine unity. That story was a rearguard action designed to champion one set of beliefs and practices over another and in order to accomplish that there had to be a good deal of invention of a normative Christian past. This book contests the idea of a single New Testament Christianity. It is organized in a way that will facilitate gaining a series of vantage points on a dynamic set of realities that occupied not only Christians, but also the millions of people who lived alongside them. In order to set the stage for that discussion, a general overview of the rise of Rome as a world power must first be sketched.

THE ROMAN WORLD: A BASIC SKETCH

Like "the New Testament," the phrase "the Roman world" masks as much as it describes. It is as impossible to speak simplistically of the Roman world as it is to talk about "the West" or "the Orient." The empire of Rome of the first two centuries CE was populated by approximately forty-five to sixty million people—roughly 85% of them rural—spread across 6.5 million square kilometers (2.5 million square miles; see map, frontispiece), who represented diverse economic and social strata, following differing customs and religious traditions, speaking hundreds of different languages, with cultures that preceded Roman rule by centuries and even, as in the case of Jewish tradition, millennia. The vast majority of people in the Roman world were more concerned with daily survival than with who was ruling the capital at any given time. It falls outside the scope of this book to present a detailed account of Rome's expansion. The following offers a sketch of Rome's gradual domination of the Mediterranean basin and extended territories in order to furnish a general orientation to the chapters that follow.

The legacy of the Greek Macedonian general and ruler Alexander the Great (356–323 BCE) is very important for understanding the organization and successful administration of the Roman Empire. Beginning in 334, Alexander began a conquest of the eastern Mediterranean, and in 326 he invaded India. In the period that Alexander was expanding his empire eastward, the city of Rome was making its presence felt in the West. At the time of Alexander, Rome was an urban republic governed by a senate. By the end of the fourth century BCE, Rome ruled Italy. During the third and second centuries BCE, it extended its dominion west to Spain, south to North Africa, and east to Greece and Asia Minor. By the middle of the first century BCE, it was the ruling power over the Mediterranean basin. As it expanded, it increasingly came into contact with the cultural legacy of Greece promoted by Alexander the Great and his successors. As he conquered the eastern Mediterranean, Alexander introduced a number of new things: the foundation of Greek colonies and the political renovation of already existing cities, the implementation of consistent political and administrative structures, the establishment of a common Greek language, shared cultural values and ideals spread among ruling aristocrats, a characteristic "international" style of architecture and iconography, and a network of trade and inter-urban relationships. After his death, Alexander's empire was divided among his chief generals, with the result that these elements were preserved and further developed. The broad terms "Hellenistic Empire" and "Hellenism" are used to describe all these features.

As Rome came to dominate the eastern Mediterranean, it found in the Greek world a ready-made set of institutions with which to govern. Part of the genius of Roman administration was its ability to absorb, reconfigure, and deploy preexisting institutions and cultures in ways that advanced its own geopolitical interests. In part, it achieved this feat by allying itself with the aristocracies and wealthy landowners who governed cities, many of them founded or conquered by Alexander and his successors. In return for allegiance to Rome, elites could continue to enjoy local power and aristocratic privileges and gain new benefits from the emperor. POLITICS!!

During the first century BCE, a complicated series of political allegiances and counter-allegiances by leading families in the city of Rome resulted in the emergence of rule by a single dynasty. In 31 BCE, at the naval Battle of Actium off the coast of northwestern Greece, Octavian was victorious over his rival, Marcus Antonius. This is an important date—first, because it ended decades of political strife in the capital, and second, because it resulted in the end of the Roman Republic and the emergence of an emperor and empire. Following his victory at Actium, Octavian returned to Rome, where the Senate awarded him the honorific title "Princeps" (First Citizen, therefore his rule is often designated as the Principate). A few years later, the Senate granted him another honorific title, Augustus ("revered," "exalted"). The "Augustan Age" refers to the years of his rule (27 BCE–14 CE). After a series of failed experiments to establish a successor, Augustus arranged for Tiberius, his adopted son, to succeed him, thus creating dynastic rule. Tiberius ruled until 37

CE, followed by Gaius, who was nicknamed Caligula (37–41), Claudius (41–54) and Nero (54–68). All of these were Augustus's relatives and members of the Julian and Claudian aristocratic families. They are accordingly named Julio-Claudian emperors. Nero committed suicide in 68; his death marks the end of the dynasty. Paul composed his first letter, to the Thessalonians, when Augustus's great nephew Claudius was the emperor, and a decade later he wrote his Epistle to the Romans when another great nephew, Nero, was emperor. Acts 18:26 refers to the expulsion of Jews from Rome by Claudius, which happened in 49 CE. Nero set fire to the capital in 64 CE to make room for a new palace he wanted to build, placing the blame on Christians, whom he then persecuted. Traditionally, the deaths of Peter and Paul are linked with Nero and his persecution, and a good deal of legend and apocryphal Christian literature developed to describe the apostles' encounters with the emperor and their eventual martyrdom.

During the year following Nero's suicide, civil war destroyed much of the city of Rome, as competing armies sought to take control of it. In 69 the senator and general T. Flavius Vespasianus emerged victorious and inaugurated a new dynasty, named after his clan name, Flavius. Vespasian and his elder son, Titus, were the generals delegated by Nero to quash the revolt in Roman Palestine known as the Jewish War (66–74). Vespasian ruled for a decade, Titus ruled from 79 to 81, and Vespasian's younger son, Domitian, ruled from 81 to 96, when he was assassinated. Many scholars, including this author, locate the majority of New Testament writings during this Flavian period. These are the four Gospels, Acts, Hebrews, James, 1 Peter, 1, 2, and 3 John, Jude, and the Book of Revelation, plus a number of letters (Colossians, Ephesians, 1– 2 Timothy, Titus, and 2 Thessalonians) written in Paul's name but, because of distinctive vocabulary and content, arguably not by the apostle himself. This book assumes that Paul did not write them and that they are evidence of pseudonymity. The widespread ancient practice of writing in the name of a celebrated teacher is also found in the Hebrew Bible (e.g., the Book of Daniel, composed in the 160s BCE), as well as a vast body of Christian and Jewish literature contemporary with the New Testament. While most scholars accept a later set of dates for these writings, some argue that the entire New Testament should be assigned to the period prior to Nero's death in 68 CE.

Following the murder of Domitian in 96, after a brief rule by Nerva, Trajan (Nerva's adopted son) ruled from 98 to 117. Trajan extended the empire to its furthest geographical reach. After winning decisive battles in Persia (contemporary Iran and Iraq), he planned to repeat Alexander's feat of invading India, but resistance from his army forced him to abandon his plan. From 116 to 117 Trajan also suppressed a protracted revolt of Jews in Cyrenaica (eastern Libya), Egypt, Cyprus, Mesopotamia, and possibly Judea. After Trajan's death, his adopted son Hadrian ruled from 117 to 138. Hadrian is important for several reasons. First, he set the boundaries for Rome's vast territorial domain, which remained until the end of the century. Second, he suppressed a third and last rebellion of Palestinian Jews, the Bar Kokhba revolt (132—36). The Jewish defeat resulted in the diaspora of the Jews from Palestine and the foundation of Jerusalem as Aelia Capitolina (after Jupiter Capitolinus, the chief deity of Rome). Hadrian prohibited Jews from entering the city and renamed Judea as Syria Palestina. Some scholars argue there are New Testament writings that come from this later period—it has been recently proposed that Acts in the form we have today was not created until the reign of Hadrian, and some place 1–2 Timothy and Titus here as well, while 2 Peter is often assigned to this period or later.

Taken as whole, the period from Augustus in 27 BCE to that of Hadrian and beyond represents rule by successive stable dynasties that established a political framework for consistent rule until the middle of the third century. In due course, the term "Rome" came to describe both the city and its territory. In other words, Rome was coterminous with the world. All of these emperors celebrated their reigns by minting coins using words such as *Pax, Pax Romana*, or *Pax Augusta*. These terms describe the peace that Rome and the emperor brought the Mediterranean world, albeit through brutal military conquest and occupation. *Pax* in this context means pacification through diplomacy, if possible, and force, if necessary. When Paul wrote the earliest document of the New Testament canon, the first Letter to the Thessalonians (ca. 48 CE), he referred indirectly to the imperial idea of peace by quoting its slogans: "You yourselves know well, that the day of the Lord will come like a thief in the night. When people say, 'There is peace and security,' then sudden destruction will come upon them" (1 Thess. 5:3). One regularly finds the terms "peace" and "security" on coins from imperial mints celebrating Roman rule. The Thessalonian passage is dramatic for the way it rejects Roman imperial ideology in expectation of the second coming of Christ.

PRACTICING SPACES

The Roman world was more than emperors and battles, of course. It comprised people who practiced everyday life. The chapters that follow offer a means of coming to an understanding of some of the main features of those practices. Each successive chapter may be conceived as a series of increasingly smaller Russian dolls nested inside one another. Chapter 2 considers the way people in the ancient world conceived of the gods, the role of sacrifice, the cosmos, and the place of ritual in daily life. Chapter 3 considers the emperor and the empire, with a focus on the imperial cult, the Roman provincial administration, and the role of benefaction and patronage in the practices of government. Chapter 4 continues the treatment of politics by taking up the organization and population of ancient cities, with a special focus on artisans, since many early Christians were probably tradespeople and merchants. The discussion then turns to households and their members in chapter 5. This chapter is pertinent because of the role of domestic structures in shaping behavior and furnishing the spaces for daily life. The final chapter considers ideas about the self in the ancient world by discussing medical views of the body, the construction of gender, ethics, and some of the leading philosophical theories about self-regulation and their relation to cosmological beliefs.

All of these phenomena, whether considered at the macro- or micro-social level, represent dynamic and intertwined social realities that can be abstracted from one another for the purposes of discussion, but which were lived as an integrated whole. People were individuals, household members, city and rural dwellers, inhabitants of the Roman Empire, and practitioners of religion with beliefs about the gods and the cosmos all at the same time. Nevertheless, it is helpful to distinguish these as a series of empirical, imagined, and practiced spaces that differed from situation to situation. To put it differently, the way people think about and act in the world differs according to the particular social spaces they find themselves within and the changing roles they play from place to place and time to time. The way one thinks, imagines, and behaves when worshiping or meditating is different from what one does when cooking a meal, voting in an election, working, and so on. Each chapter considers the ways in which empirical realities, ways of interpreting and imagining the world, and patterns of practice worked together to create spaces that groups and individuals inhabited variously, depending on a variety of factors that include such things as religious ritual, civic identity, domestic location, socioeconomic status, and gender.

The French social geographer Michel de Certeau, in a study of what he called "the practices of everyday life," offered a helpful way of conceiving the way early Christians inhabited each of the contexts the following chapters describe.[6] The term "practices" describes routine activities such as cooking, reading, walking, talking, and so on. He used the terms "strategies" and "tactics" to describe the way people practice everyday life. Strategies are represented by the institutions and structures created for the organization and regulation of daily life. City planners, for example, create sidewalks to mark where pedestrians are to travel as they move from one point to another, to facilitate the safe flow of traffic, and to mark boundaries that divide public and private spaces. Individuals, however, may walk along the same sidewalk at different speeds and in differing ways, or someone might cut across a street and jaywalk. Or, more dramatically, someone might use a sidewalk to create street art or spray a piece of graffiti. Certeau used the term "tactics" to describe improvisations of strategies for particular social aims. He saw the practice of daily life as a font for creativity and possibilities of social improvisation and even power disruption.

Certeau's theorization of daily practice, strategies, and tactics is especially useful for the study of Christian belief and practice in the context of the Roman world. We should imagine believers occupying themselves with daily life in accordance with cosmic, imperial, civic, and familial strategies that came with being a part of the social order and that were used and promoted by those in control of society in ways that assured their power and position. However, at particular moments, in certain conditions, and in specific places, beliefs resulted in creative tactics that modified—perhaps one should say twisted—preexisting codes in novel ways. For example, the Book of Revelation uses the language of the cult of the Roman emperor to describe the lordship of Jesus as a means to promote Christian resistance to the ideology of the imperial cult.

At other times, Christians appropriated preexisting strategies in more conservative ways to limit improvisation and creativity. First Timothy, for example, by forbidding women to have authority over men and commanding them to remain silent and bear children, sought to limit the ways some women were probably using Paul's teachings to reject traditional household roles. These examples illustrate ways in which the writings of the New Testament were composed in the context of larger strategies of social organization and codes of behavior.

It is important to remember that each New Testament writing expresses its own constellation of practices and beliefs. These documents do not offer a timelessly true set of coordinates that can be used simplistically to understand the ancient world or to guide contemporary behavior. Nor were they composed with a view to being interpreted by other writings found in the canon. Each represents its own situation and set of interests. By attending to ideas and practices related to the cosmos and religion, the empire, the city, the household, and the self, we place the New Testament within a dynamic, interconnected set of realities in an attempt to understand more fully the emergence of a new religion in the Roman world.

A BRIEF NOTE ON NOMENCLATURE

For the sake of convenience, I have been using the terms "Christianity," "Christian," "Judaism," and "Jew." These terms refer to dynamic and unfolding phenomena of the ancient world. The risk in using them is to reify ancient data into stable notions, and then use those concepts as tools for interpretation of the material under consideration, thereby creating a vicious feedback loop. The New Testament represents a host of independently formed and chronologically varied ideas that would later be drawn upon to theorize and promote a religion we today call "Christianity," with a set of doctrines, rituals, codes of conduct, and so on. The content of Christian belief was largely settled by the fifth century, but it continues to be debated by contemporary Christian traditions, theologians, and scholars of religion. In order to represent an earlier period of religious emergence, some scholars thus prefer the language of "Christ believer" and "Christ religion" to "Christian" and "Christianity." When these terms are used in what follows, they are meant to designate an unfolding set of realities. Further, while there is a utility in speaking of "Jews" and "Christians" in the ancient world, the evidence points to an entangled set of beliefs, practices, and rituals in the first centuries of the Common Era, and some argue that what today we call Judaism and Christianity only emerged as separable traditions as late as the fourth century. The use of the two terms in what follows should not be understood as indicative of a clear separation of two self-defined religions. Finally, as in the case of "Christian" and "Christianity," "Jew" and "Judaism" represent a set of religious, ethnic, and social phenomena that were in the first centuries CE as much under construction as beliefs centered on Jesus of Nazareth. Some scholars seek to delimit the use of the last two terms to later centuries and instead use the terms "Ioudaios," "Ioudaioi," and "Ioudaian," to capture the ethnicity of Judaism and its demographic definition in the first centuries of the Common Era. The distinction is meant to draw attention to an ethnicity derived from a shared geographical origin, set of customs and rituals, and sometimes language, rather than a self-defined "religion" codified in practices and rituals. By linking religious identity with an ethnos or people, Judaism was not different from other geographically and ethnically defined religious devotions practiced by the many peoples of the Roman Empire. Some scholars mistakenly argue that Jewish religious association with ethnicity was in some way a special case of separatist identity and even arrogance in the Roman world. In this view, Christian "grace" is the antidote to Jewish "race."[7] Such an idea has a long legacy, with roots going back to Martin Luther's obscene disparaging of Jews and centuries of Christian teachings that discredit Judaism as a retrograde religion. There is not space in this book to trace the many ways in which some leading New Testament scholars perpetuate this point of view. Suffice it to say that, by the use of "Christian" and "Jew," this book in no way seeks to endorse such ideas. The following discussion uses these terms as shorthand expressions for the sake of convenience. However, the dynamic and context-specific nature that determined not only *what* defined belief and practice, but also *when* belief and practice were determinative of identity, and in *which* situations, means that the terms "Jews," "Christians," "Judaism," and "Christianity" refer to an inchoate reality in the period under consideration here.

THE GODS AND

THE COSMOS

Little children, keep yourselves from idols.

—*1 John 5:21*

THE FOREIGN WORLD OF ANCIENT RELIGION

When we turn to consider the gods of the New Testament period and the people who worshiped them, we find ourselves in a foreign world. In most modern societies, religion is a matter of private belief separated from the public world of politics, economics, law, and so on. The United States goes so far as to enshrine the separation of church and state in its constitution. We use the term "secular" to describe a social order that restricts religion from the operation of public society and confines it to private domains. Secular also refers to people who live their daily lives without reference to God or anything religious. Today, when people describe themselves as "atheist," "agnostic," or "spiritual but not religious," they are confirming a basic secular point of view.

There was no such thing as the secular in the world of the New Testament. The peoples inhabiting the Roman world did not separate religious beliefs and practices from public life, nor did they confine them to private piety. Religion was embedded in all aspects of society, including such things as economics, politics, the administration of justice, the conduct of war, and public festivities, as well as everything one did in private life. This embedded religion is a theme to which we will return repeatedly in this book, since we can scarcely talk about the New Testament and its social worlds without constant reference to religion at all levels of life. Indeed, New Testament writers often strive to exert control over various aspects of the daily lives of Christians, both inside the home and outside it. The most graphic example of this competition is the Book of Revelation, where John criticizes believers who are involved too much in the economic life of the Roman Empire and not dedicated enough to Christ. However, we find it all the way through the New Testament, as we will see in this chapter and the ones that follow.

As belief in Jesus developed into an imperial religion that would eventually spread throughout the Roman Empire, the question of whether, how, where, and when Christians could participate in society became relevant for an increasing number of the empire's inhabitants. From the point of view of several early Jesus followers, believers were to refuse to take part in certain events and public practices associated with deities. For example, sculptors and painters who made or painted idols could not be part of the church.[1] Others forbade Christians to attend popular entertainments like the theater or the gladiatorial contests and other games of the arena.[2] Attendance at such events was forbidden not only because they were dedicated to particular deities, but also because divine images were present where they were hosted. However, to make these kinds of restrictions was to open a Pandora's box. In the cities where Christianity developed, images of the gods were found in shops, in taverns, at baths, in various rooms of a household ranging from the kitchen to dining room to the bed chamber, at street corners, at school—almost anywhere one looked. How were Christians to interpret this world? If believers were accustomed to the worship of the gods and then became followers of a religion that renounced the worship or display of these images, how were they now going to live? People were used to religious practices dedicated to many different gods, depending on the occasion and social rituals, like banqueting with friends and colleagues, giving gifts at certain religious celebrations, hanging garlands, and rites of passage, as well as citywide celebrations such as processions when everyone took part in festivities. It would have been both challenging and socially isolating for converts to Christianity to absent themselves from these things. While nonparticipation would have been scarcely noticeable to the larger public, it would certainly have made one immediately conspicuous to unbelieving family members and neighbors, and would possibly have raised questions about proper concern for the public good. The complexities were only magnified when a New Testament writer like Paul expressly instructed his audience *not* to break off relations with "the immoral of this world, or the greedy and robbers, or idolaters, since you would then need to go out of the world" (1 Cor. 5:10). Christians would wrestle with this issue for centuries; many still do.

The belief of ancients in many gods is another challenge for people hoping to understand the social world of the New Testament. For the modern secular person, one of the chief questions religion raises is whether or not there is a God. Some in the ancient world questioned the existence of the gods, but they were rare. The chief interest of most people was not whether there were gods, but which god or what ritual was the one needed to get what they wanted or to get answers to pressing questions like whether one should get married or not, what a dream meant, how to assure success at business, or what was going to happen in the future. It was easier for people in antiquity to believe that there was no god than that there was only one. For them, not only were there many gods, but more were awaiting discovery. In the Book of Acts, Paul tries to capitalize on this belief in as yet unknown gods (Acts 17:16–34). When he goes to Athens, he is dismayed at the number of "idols" (statues and images of gods, altars, temples, and so on) he sees there (v. 16). He meets with Athenians at the Areopagus, a place where the citizens assembled, and he begins his speech by pointing to a public altar dedicated to "a god unknown" (v. 23). Paul tries to convince his audience that the unknown deity is in fact the one God of Israel revealed in the Hebrew Bible and is the only God who should be worshiped.

The structure of ancient society made Paul's speech difficult to accept (Acts 17:32–34). In addition to the routine social rituals involving the images the apostle rejected, people engaged in countless different religious practices dedicated to the various deities themselves. There were formal, regular public rituals to assure the well-being of the state, and there were private, elective rituals for personal needs like healing toothaches. State officials performed certain rituals when they went to war and when they made peace. Various rituals—some public, some private—might be performed at the turn of the seasons, on special days of festivities, on each day of the week, in the morning and in the evening, and at mealtimes. People used rituals to curse neighbors, to cast love spells, and to protect themselves from the curses and spells of others. Although nobody engaged in all of this all of the time, and practices varied among Greeks and Romans, the fact remains that ritual was an integral part of everyday life.

A further challenge in understanding ancient religion relates to the modern notion of "belief" in God. Ancients, of course, believed in and had many beliefs about the gods, but belief in the modern religious sense of the term was not their chief interest. There were no formal doctrinal systems of the kind found in Christianity. People spoke as easily about "god" as they did about "the gods." They could talk about Zeus as though he was one god among many, or they could see the many gods as differing aspects of one divine reality or power. This is the reason why referring to the "polytheism" of the ancient world, as opposed to the "monotheism" of Judaism, Christianity, and Islam, can produce a misleading distinction. This book avoids these terms.

Closely related to the question of belief is the practice of ritual. In matters of religion, modern people, who believe a personal relationship with God to be the mark of true faith, are quick to condemn "empty ritual." This relatively recent distinction is largely a product of the Christian movements of reform and renewal from the Reformation onward. For the civic elites, sincerity or a personal relationship with a god or gods was not a determining feature in the religious world of the New Testament. What was important was knowing how to use the divine world, how to ask the gods or spirits (in Greek, *daimones*) to do or ensure something, or to refrain from doing something, and how to obtain authoritative information about a present or future situation by means of one of dozens of different kinds of divination. Right performance was the critical issue, not whether one was sincere in performing a ritual. However, this is not to say that sincerity was wholly unimportant to ancient people (or the gods, for that matter), or that people did not have or seek religious experiences. Some religions were attractive because they offered powerful religious experiences. One form of religion, the mystery cults, included an elaborate set of rituals through which one experienced union with a god. Nevertheless, sincerity and personal experience were not the central categories of ancient religion. People *did* things with respect to the gods. They were not so much "believers" in religion as practitioners of it.

A further critical difference from modern religious belief is the importance in antiquity of beneficial social exchange between people of different status. The particular form of such exchange that is important here is patronage. Patronage can be described as the glue that held the social order of the Roman

Empire together. Social inferiors, lacking material assets, offered respect, deference, honor, and service to social superiors in return for the more tangible benefits of food, cash, gifts, jobs, and power. This model of social relations was applied to the divine world and institutionalized as votive religion. The individual, in a situation of stress, danger, illness, need, or ambition, promises a specific gift if the god addressed performs the boon requested. If the god answers or is deemed to have answered the request, the beneficiary is obliged to fulfill the vow. We can also describe votive religion as a form of gift exchange between unequal parties (asymmetrical gift exchange). This type of exchange is a topic to which we will return repeatedly in this book, in part because it is a recurring New Testament theme, but more importantly because it suffused relations at all levels of society.

The opposite was also believed—that deities could be destructive when angered or slighted by sacrifices and rituals that were neglected or incorrectly performed. Rituals were also designed to repair relations with gods. In a world filled with illness, poverty, crime, exploitation, and conflict, people were constantly menaced by forces outside their control. Religion offered a way for individuals, groups, and larger collective bodies like cities or even an emperor and his empire to rationalize what was happening around them, to anticipate future events, and to have some control over their outcome. When there were severe collective disasters like earthquakes, epidemics, crop failures, famine, or military defeat, the first thing people tended to ask was what they had done to anger or disappoint the gods. We can see this concern at work in a dispute described in Acts 19:21–41. When Paul is preaching his Gospel in Ephesus and urging his audience to renounce the worship of idols, Demetrius sees him as a menace to public safety and to his livelihood as owner of a workshop producing miniature shrines in precious metal for worshippers to offer to Artemis, the patron deity of the city.

"There is danger" he says, "not only that this trade of ours may come into disrepute but also that the temple of the great goddess Artemis will be scorned, and she will be deprived of her majesty that brought all Asia and the world to worship her" (v. 27). Demetrius believes that a scorned goddess is an angry and punishing one.

GODS AND THE COSMOS

With these critical distinctions in mind, we are ready to tackle what people in antiquity thought about the gods and the cosmos and what they believed when they worshiped them. How did people contemporary with the New Testament understand the cosmos in which they lived and the god or gods who ruled it? Ancients did not have a book like the Bible to learn about revelation from the gods. What they had was the world around them and their experiences, which, of course, they interpreted in terms of the religious ideas current in their own rural area, village, town, or city. Almost all of these practices were passed on orally—people learned their religious practices by imitating those around them, and they learned their religious ideas by listening to stories about the gods and spirits ("myths"), some of them passed down from time immemorial, adapted to current circumstances. More educated people, especially in cities in the Greek-speaking eastern Mediterranean, knew, and could even quote from, a few, long, poetic texts like Homer's *Iliad* and *Odyssey* and Hesiod's *Theogony* and *Works and Days* (both written in the eighth century BCE), which were believed, because they were so ancient, to contain valuable information about the deities. Religious experts like priests and soothsayers helped communities and individuals to determine the gods' will in order to try to assure good fortune. When bad things happened, these specialists were again on hand to find the cause and thus give advice on the way to restore good relations with the gods.

At a quite different social level, among the privileged, educated elites, philosophical systems developed cosmologies (structured accounts of the order and meaning of the cosmos), which included the divine power or powers that they believed governed the universe. Philosophers who lived in the centuries before Christ, such as Plato, Aristotle, and the Stoics, developed cosmologies that had a profound influence on the more educated people of the Roman Empire and their understanding of the gods and the universe. All of them imagined a single divinity as ultimately responsible for the order of the universe; that is, they were philosophical "monotheists." Where possible, they reinterpreted (or simply ignored) the stories of the gods to fit into their systems of thought. Such ideas had only an indirect effect on the mostly illiterate population.

People in antiquity learned about the gods and their roles in the way the cosmos worked at their mother's knee through constantly changing oral narratives, some of which were widely known, but most of which only circulated locally or regionally. Since we are here thinking mainly of the eastern (Greek-speaking) Mediterranean area, we can focus on Greek stories, although, of course, there were innumerable non-Greek peoples in this vast area, with their own traditions, almost none of which have survived. An essential part of ancient Greek culture was a shared set of Olympian gods, later made into a more or less standardized list of twelve deities, and stories about them. Some ancient people, feeling there must be more to them than the mere narratives, read them as symbolic stories containing timeless truths about life and death or forces of nature. Many ancient philosophers interpreted them as eternal truths about a single divinity or a divine power or quality inherent in the cosmos. However, to the people of the everyday world where New Testament authors and their audiences lived, these were not allegories masking deeper meanings. Most people took it for granted that the gods really existed and that the stories told about them were true. At the same time, it was perfectly possible to find the stories, and indeed the gods, ridiculous. In the second century CE, the satirical writer Lucian of Samosata wrote numerous burlesques showing the gods moaning about how little people cared for them.

The average uneducated Greek probably imagined the world as a flat disk surrounded by a great river, Oceanus. Above the disk was a bowl-shaped sky, and below it was Hades, which contained several compartments and rivers, and to which there were quite a number of supposed entrances. One of the most important underworld rivers was the Styx, which ordinary people, once they died, crossed after paying the ferryman, Charon. Broadly speaking, the main gods were divided into two groups. There were the twelve—more or less, depending on who was counting—"Olympian" deities (so-called because Homer set them in a sort of palace on Mount Olympus, a real mountain in northern Greece), and a very uncertain number of chthonic deities or entities who inhabited the underworld (*chthôn* is one ancient Greek word for earth, and *chthonios* the corresponding adjective, "of the earth"). The chief Olympians were Zeus, the Top God who ruled the sky, and Poseidon, who governed the sea. Hades (or Pluto) and Persephone, together with Hecate, controlled the underworld. The chief differences between gods and humans were that gods were immortal, immeasurably more powerful, could be in many places at once, and were in a position to bestow unlimited benefits. However, in many other respects, they were very similar to human beings—they might have human shape, and they were thought to need food and drink, have a substance analogous to blood in their bodies, and feel emotions very similar to human ones.

The exact list of names included in the local pantheon, and their relative importance, differed from place to place. At

Athens, for example, Athena was the major divinity; at Corinth, Apollo; and at Ephesus, Artemis. Still, everyone in each community knew the names of the major local gods, how they came about, how they were related, where they lived, and some of the things they were supposed to have done. An inexhaustibly varied and constantly developing array of stories developed around these deities. People took special pride in narratives recounting events relating to their own city or vicinity. Such stories confirmed the special relationship between locality and deity, which could reasonably be projected into the future. Places where epiphanies/appearances of the god had occurred were marked by means of altars and temples and were commemorated by regular festivals. Divinities prominent in local myths were often also represented in statuary, which might be brought out in solemn procession at festivals, and the narratives in which they featured were reproduced visually in relief sculpture. Such images played a vital part in stabilizing the collective imagination regarding the appearance and even the identity of the major gods, and so fed back into people's dreams and private imaginings.

If we now look beyond Olympus, there were uncountable numbers of lesser deities. The ancient world was thick with divine powers in a way that is scarcely comprehensible to modern people. Moreover, there were innumerable slight differences of opinion about their parentage, location, and responsibilities. Some came into being when the children and grandchildren of the Olympians produced other, lesser gods, or when (male) gods had intercourse with human females. Among them were many "personifications," or divinized principles, of which the most important were the Charites (the Graces)—usually three females personifying beauty, elegance, and pleasure. Often associated with Aphrodite, they were present at all joyful events of both humans and gods. There were also the Hours and the nine female Muses who presided over the arts. They sang for the gods and inspired all human intellectual endeavors. Pan, the god of the wild mountain, of shepherds and flocks, might cause sudden fright (hence the English word "panic"). Natural phenomena like stars, winds, and rivers were thought of as gods. Caves, springs, trees, and groves might be inhabited by nymphs (and Pan), who were bound to particular places and, although long-lived, were believed to be ultimately mortal. There were also many more or less horrible and threatening divine figures, such as the Erinyes (the Furies), who avenged crimes and were later associated with the underworld. All of these "intermediate" or minor deities enjoyed the dignity of having a more or less distinctive iconography devised for them.

This was not the case, however, for a still lower form of divinity, the innumerable, unnamed *daimones* (sing. *daimôn*). Whereas in the Homeric period, there was no clear-cut distinction between the gods and *daimones*, Plato (428/27—348/47 BCE) assigned them to an intermediate position between deities and humans. They came to be understood as semidivine spirit guides, who could influence people to certain actions, good or bad, as in the case of Socrates's inner moral voice (his *daimonion*); some people believed that each person had his or her own *daimôn*, which steered one's particular destiny or fate. These *daimones* are not to be confused with Judeo-Christian "demons," although the Greek words are the same. The association of *daimones* with malign powers developed in the pre-Christian period as ancient Near Eastern ideas came into contact with Greek ones. In the four centuries before the Common Era, some Jews developed beliefs about them as hostile powers keeping the world in bondage. Paul reflects those currents when he reminds his audience that they are in a spiritual battle against "the principalities, against the powers, against the world rulers of this present darkness, against the spiritual hosts of wickedness in the heavenly places" (Eph. 6:12). Many early Christians and Jews counted the gods among the innumerable wicked powers that had power over creation and bent it to their evil ends. As we will see below, this sometimes took the form of a developed angelology and demonology. It also resulted in an ambiguous attitude toward Roman authorities: New Testament writers sometimes spoke positively of emperors as appointed by god to keep order (Rom. 13:1–7; 1 Tim. 2:1–2; 1 Pet. 2:13–14), but at other times they referred to them as guided by Satan and fallen angels (Rev. 12:9; 13:1–2; 20:7–10).

Finally, there were male and female heroes, who were born as mortals but because of their great deeds were given the gift of immortality. Heracles/Hercules and Asclepius/Aesculapius, who achieved full divinity, mark the upper limit of the class. But there were many more obscure ones who owed their status to political considerations, such as the founder(s) of each Greek colony. Devotees offered cult to them at a *heröon* (pl. *heroa*), which was a building or cenotaph often erected over the spot the hero was believed to have died and where his or her bones were believed to be. Unlike the Olympians, who could be everywhere, heroes could exercise their power only at the spot where they died or where their mortal remains were. As a result, there was often competition over the place the hero really died, and hence where proper cult was being offered. In the ancient world, the adult dead were buried outside the city walls, but *heroa* were often located inside the city. They were also built at approaches to cities, along its territorial frontiers, or at city gates. One of their roles was to protect the population from invasion.

Heroes raise another important issue with regard to ancient religion. For accomplishing great tasks, the gods rewarded humans with divinity. Usually the award was given posthumously, but sometimes people claimed divine power when they were still alive. For example, if a general won a battle or if a woman was particularly beautiful, people might celebrate him or her as manifesting divine power. This is an important theme we will return to when we discuss the role of emperor worship in the

Roman Empire. It is an idea the New Testament approximates when it affirms that because of Jesus's righteousness or faithfulness to God, God has exalted him to divine sonship (Phil. 2:6–11; Rom. 1:3–4; Acts 2:29–36; Heb. 1:3–4). Some argue that these texts attest that the human Jesus was divinized on account of his achievement. Others suggest that they reflect rather the full revelation of Jesus's divinity in his resurrection, or that they celebrate his elevation to supreme authority. The point here is that there was nothing novel or exotic about making these kinds of claims about Jesus. Such ideas were part of the basic cultural understanding of the way gods and the world interacted.

People in antiquity viewed the gods anthropomorphically; that is, they thought of them as looking like humans and having human characteristics. Each god possessed certain character qualities believed to typify him or her, which resulted in idiosyncratic behaviors and hence assignment to different kinds of tasks. They could be associated with leading human virtues like wisdom or courage, or with skills like military prowess and hunting. They also possessed a colorful family history marked by squabbles, intermarriage, adultery, incest, jealousies, betrayals, and a series of complicated relationships with humans. Later Christian writers reveled in recounting the tales of the unseemly behavior of these gods, which they thought proved not only the immorality of pagan deities, but also the perversity of worshiping them. They hoped thereby to prove the moral superiority of the Christian God and His followers. Another ploy was to point out the contradictory claims made about any single deity. Part of the appeal of such criticism must have been that in a world with so much uncertainty it scarcely helped to trust in a set of gods so subject to foibles, human weaknesses, and inconsistency. Jews and Christians who attempted to defend their religion against their opponents were quick to point to how their God, as a singular deity, was not vying for attention with a set of poorly behaving gods. The behavior one could expect from their God was unfailingly just and good, they argued. The Bible provided a revelation of a God who was consistent, trustworthy, and loving. There one found nothing of the shenanigans found in the tales of the Greek and Roman gods.

Although worshipers of the Greek and Roman gods would have agreed with their Christian opponents that their deities were complex and capricious, it is doubtful that many would have found the Christians' criticisms any more persuasive than those of the philosophers. It is important to understand that Christian criticism missed an important point. Objections based on the personalities and adventures of the gods leave the impression that the gods could be reduced to static labels, qualities, or personality profiles. But gods were powers as much as they were persons or personalities. Differing cultic contexts and narrative traditions resulted in people focusing on a god's aspects and potencies. When viewing the gods from this angle, it is better to speak of a portfolio of different functions and powers divided among the deities than to describe them as distinct persons. Although the name of a god pointed to a specific deity, it functioned as an umbrella term that could include a whole series of names, qualities, the melding of two or more deities, and so on. It is for this reason that, while Greeks generally talked in terms of many gods, they saw no contradiction in speaking of "god" in the singular. There was no central organizing principle to structure a divinity's personality and actions. Gods were multifaceted with a wide variety of titles, and the religion dedicated to them was, as a consequence, dynamic and unsystematic.

This dynamic aspect is seen in the fact that ancients gave gods various epithets or titles. These named things like their qualities, their specific functions, or their places of origin or residence. Zeus, for example, could be named Zeus Keraunios (of Thunder), Zeus Xenios (of Hospitality to Strangers), Zeus Eleutherios (of Freedom), Zeus Ombrios (of Rain), Zeus

Teleios (of Marriage), or Zeus Soter (who saved or will save us from a danger)—to name only a few. He was also named Zeus Olympios, Zeus of Laodicea, and Zeus Lydios, after places where he enjoyed distinctive cult. Thus, a single Zeus and innumerable Zeuses were present in the same moment. Differing divine epithets furnished different avenues of communication with the deity. One could approach Zeus Teleios to ask for a happy marriage or Zeus Ombrios to request rain.

Given this view of gods, each rich with multiple capabilities, one can see how that which Christians and Jews criticized as a vice of inconsistency on the part of the gods could be turned on its head and understood as a paramount virtue of ancient religion. It opened many avenues of approach to the deities and their manifold benefits. For example, because she was associated with love, people called on Aphrodite to create irresistible passion in an otherwise unavailable partner. However, since she was the lover of Ares, the god of war, she was also called upon to inspire a city's army with warlike fury in battling its enemies. As she was born from the sea, sailors worshiped her as the patron goddess of navigation. Aphrodite was both one and many. When we realize that every god shared the same range of possibilities, we see how complex the world of ancient religion was.

EPIPHANIES

As one would expect in a world full of gods and spirits, events of many kinds could be interpreted as encounters with deities. Such "god-events" could occur anywhere and at any time. When gods appeared, humans offered sacrifice. The story in Acts 14:8–14 of a healing performed by Barnabas and Paul at the city of Lystra in southern Asia Minor furnishes an illustration of this. Upon witnessing the wonder, the Lystrans hail them as the Olympian deities Zeus and Hermes. "The gods have come down to us in the likeness of men," they exclaim (14:11). They saw the apostles as epiphanies or physical appearances of the gods. The first thing the Lystrans wanted to do was to offer sacrifices to them (vv. 13, 18). This story is an excellent snapshot of ancient religious belief in action. First, we see that the Lystrans believed that the gods were not remote, but close by. They expressed the popular belief amongst everyday people that the gods could show up at any moment and do miraculous things. They watched what people were doing, and they rewarded and punished them according to their deserts. Second, we see how people turned to ritual to honor the gods' epiphany and thereby enter into a relationship of gift exchange with them. The priest of Zeus brings oxen and garlands to offer sacrifice with the people (v. 13). Third, we can see competition over which divinity should be honored. Here, as elsewhere in the New Testament, it is through divine power that the apostles accomplish signs and wonders. The question is not whether such mighty deeds can happen, but which divinity or cosmic power is responsible for them. In the story from Acts, the apostles urge the Lystrans to abandon "worthless things" and turn "to a living God who made heaven and the earth and all that is in them" (v. 15). Their claim is that the most powerful god, the one God to whom all should offer worship and religious service, is not Zeus or any Olympian, but their God, Jesus.

In a world of divine epiphanies where people could believe that Zeus might show up as Paul and Barnabas, they would not have been surprised to learn that Christians believed that the fullness of God dwelt bodily in Jesus (Col. 2:9), or that they taught that Jesus is "the reflection of God's glory and the exact imprint of God's very being" (Heb. 1.3). When people heard Jesus described as the epiphany (appearing) of God (2 Thess. 2:8; 1 Tim. 6:14; 2 Tim. 1:10; 4.1, 8; Titus 2:13), they would have been familiar with a host of places, people, and stories associated with the epiphanies of Greek gods. It is also true that references to God's epiphanies also occur in the Hebrew Bible.

The point here is not to exclude one understanding in favor of another, but rather to recognize the resonance of such belief in a world where people believed the gods regularly appeared.

Unsurprising, as well, would have been the belief that the raised Jesus could be present in several places at once, both in heaven and on earth. If various gods of the Roman pantheon could do it, it would seem reasonable that he could. What *would* have been surprising to worshipers of the gods was that they should dedicate themselves to this deity *alone*. Further, while divine powers were believed to settle on certain extraordinarily gifted individuals or on some who had undergone certain initiation rites, it would nevertheless have been surprising for most people to hear some Christians claim that the divine person Jesus Christ resided with them wherever and whenever they met, and that he took up permanent residence in each believer. When Paul called the church "the body of Christ," he meant that literally: the body of believers was a gathering where the power of the divine Christ was known, was experienced, and was present. His body was simultaneously in Corinth and Rome and wherever the believers gathered.

TEMPLES

Temples, altars, and sanctuaries were the chief public places where people worshiped the gods. Cities and their surrounding countryside were filled with them. One could hardly go along a street without encountering one of these places and the images of the gods that were worshiped at them. Not all temples were identical, and the sacrifices differed depending on region, the god(s) addressed, and local customs. The Greek word for the temple precinct, the piece of land consecrated to a specific god, is *temenos* (pl. *temenê*). It could range in size from a relatively small plot on a street corner to an area large enough to contain several buildings. Greek temples took many forms. The Greek term for the actual shrine that housed the cult statue is *naos*. Typically, the *naos* was a rectangular room surrounded by colonnades, which supported a roof and stood on a platform several steps high, the whole construction being a temple. To enter it, one walked past the columns to a porch and then through a door into the main hall, where the statue was. All temples had a large sacrificial altar located in front of the shrine, on which the parts of the animals owed to the gods were burned (see Figure 2.1).

Temenê controlled by cities were generally public spaces open to everyone, irrespective of gender or status. Admission was, however, controlled and limited by purity regulations that specified who might not be admitted. Minor pollution could

FIGURE 2.1 Replica Roman temple of Jupiter, Tongeren (Atuatuca Tungrorum), Gallia Belgica, first century CE. Gallo-Romeins Museum, Belgium. Image reproduced with the permission of Jona Lendering (http://www.livius.org/contributor/jona-lendering/).

be removed on entry by washing. It is unclear whether worshipers were generally admitted to the *naos* itself, or under what conditions, but certainly sacrifice did not involve entry into the temple.

As already stated, transactions between gods and humans were based on asymmetrical gift exchange. The language of communication on the human side was sacrifices, libations, first offerings, prayer, and vows. Gods responded by granting or withholding benefits, and they punished wrongdoing by bringing misfortune. Both operated at the private as well as the public level. Libations and "thank offerings" such as offering the first fruits can be thought of as routine or customary acts of acknowledgment. Blood sacrifice was a more elaborate means of demonstrating personal or collective piety. This was a means of entering into a quasi-contractual arrangement with a deity and describes the fundamental ancient institution of the votive. The representatives of the state or the private individual would make a solemn vow to make a return—usually by some kind of sacrifice—if their request was granted.

Returns varied enormously. A major option was to make offerings to the temple of the god concerned. These might be expensive items, such as drinking vessels or jewelry made of gold; goblets, plate, or statuettes in silver; elaborate bronze ornaments; or small terra cotta figurines of various animal and human forms. In the case of successful healing, people offered *ex voto* anatomical representations of the relevant part of the body, like eyes, hands, intestines, legs, feet, or, quite often, female breasts and male and female genitalia (see Figure 2.2).

Some scholars think that anatomical votives also functioned as an indication to the god of the request. Temples could be so crowded with votive offerings that one could scarcely move among them. At a certain point, the cheap, mass-produced figurines would be cleared and ritually disposed of by priests or temple wardens in order to make room for new offerings. The

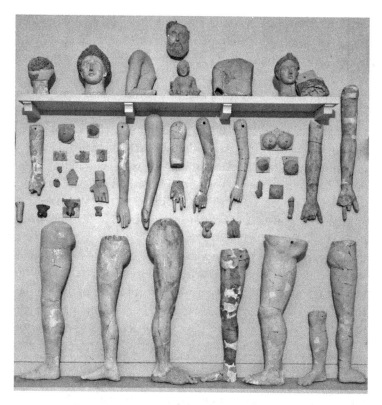

FIGURE 2.2 Terra cotta votive or *ex voto* Asclepieion figures, Corinth, first century CE. From Mabel Lang, *Cure and Cult in Ancient Corinth: A Guide to the Asklepieion*, American Excavations in Old Corinth, Corinth Notes 1, fig. 14 (Princeton: American School of Classical Studies at Athens, 1977). Photo bw_5714 courtesy of the American School of Classical Studies at Athens, Corinth Excavations.

fact that archaeologists have found them all over the Roman Empire attests both to their importance in the everyday practice of religion and to the universal language of gift exchange between people and the gods. It was also very common to respond by offering a blood sacrifice—a ram or pig, a chicken or dove, depending on one's resources, and/or to set up an altar, which might be quite elaborately carved with a (normally purely formulaic) inscription documenting the fact that that the god had answered one's request.

Votive altars were essentially decorative and mnemonic, quite unlike the grand altars built in front of temples, which were primarily functional. These functional altars took a variety of forms, ranging from stones or turf-sods piled on top of one another to highly elaborate structures decorated with reliefs. However, most were extended tables, often several meters long, built of stone or brick, on which select parts of sacrificial animals were burned. It was near the altar that libations were poured and the animals were killed and butchered. The parts of the animals reserved for the priests, and other gifts such as small cakes, fruit, and wine, offered to the deity were piled onto "tables" of metal or wood and placed inside the *naos* of the temple.

Sacrifices were made to win the gods' patronage, to keep the terms of a vow, to ensure continuing good fortune, as in the case of harvest offerings, or to give thanks. Sacrifices were also made to win back a god's favor when an individual, group, or city suffered misfortune. In civic contexts the person making the sacrifice was either an officeholder (conventionally termed "magistrates" by ancient historians) or a priest of a public cult. It did not require the presence of a priest to make these offerings, because in Greek and Roman antiquity, priesthood was not a profession requiring special qualification, but an office, an aspect of public life. Indeed, there were no rules about who might offer sacrifice, and, if we think in terms of absolute numbers, heads of households conducted the majority of sacrifices. It was thus impossible for sacrificial rituals to follow a set form, though there was a general pattern. Greek ritual (which differed significantly from Roman forms, not discussed here) included a libation of wine poured, burning of incense at a portable altar, and an animal sacrifice. The latter involved the ritual killing of the animal, performed by professional butchers, bleeding it out and smearing its blood on the altar, skinning and cutting it into parts, and the sacrificer and a small number of other privileged persons then eating some of the offal (the heart, liver, lungs, pancreas) roasted over the altar. Other parts were burned to the god; the usual open-air location of alters allowed for the smoke and pleasing smell of the roasted meat to rise to the god. The local temple rules specified which additional parts were reserved for the priests (where they were involved). The red meat was then cooked (boiled and/or roasted) and eaten by the sacrificer and his family, or, in the case of a civic sacrifice, it was eaten by the magistrates and public priests in dining rooms attached to the temple. Otherwise, it might be saved and served at banquets that would take place in the temple at a later time. Any leftover meat would subsequently be sold in the market, a practice Paul alludes to in his discussion of eating meat at an unbeliever's house (1 Cor. 10:25–29).

When people shared in a temple banquet of sacrificed meat, they believed that the god was present eating with them. Paul is challenging this view when he remarks that "(idol) food will not bring us close to God" (1 Cor. 8:8). He assumes this backdrop when first he advises the Corinthians not to eat dinners at temples (8:10), and then explicitly forbids it as being communion with demons (10:14–21). Even as the sacrifice marked off the divine from the human, banquets held in the temple dining rooms were an important means of marking and preserving social hierarchy and maintaining social relations. At citywide festivals, distributions of meat to citizens followed the sacrifice, but only the privileged received portions of the sacrificed animal.

In legal terms, each public temple was the property of the deity to whom it was dedicated. In practice, however, they and their moneys were administered by the city council. In the case of larger, more prominent, and/or popular, temples, such treasuries could be large and be sources of considerable city revenue. Cult officials were usually a city's leading citizens, who could (and often did) simultaneously hold political office. It was a civic honor to hold a priesthood, and its incumbent usually received the office because of benefaction. Such honor also often included the erection of a statue of the person dressed as a priest together with an inscription listing the recipient's virtues, public offices held, and benefactions to the cult and the city. These inscriptions were very important in the marking of status.

As stated at the start of this chapter, there was no distinction among religion, politics, and economics, which meant that the temple treasury could also function as a bank. Priests used it to make loans, for example, and it was at the temple that records of debt were kept. Before the eyes of the temple's god, where it was thought they would be more honest, people concluded business transactions, swore oaths, and entered into legal contracts. The god's presence at the temples also meant that the sanctuary became the place of political and judicial meetings. It was here that the public archives were stored, including records of honors and citizenship lists. Important decrees were often inscribed on the walls of temples or on stone inscriptions displayed there.

People believed that the gods resided in the their temple precincts and that their statues were visible tokens of their presence. In a way that was not systematically theorized, the images of the gods mediated their presence without, strictly speaking, being identical with them. One of the Bible's central criticisms of the worship of many gods is that it is an act of idolatry. Paul, for example, repeats a standard Jewish objection to ancient religion as the worship of idols when he talks of Gentiles fashioning images of animals and worshiping them (Rom. 1:21–23). John, in Revelation, similarly condemns the worship of images of the emperor (Rev. 13:14–15).

Idols were believed to manifest the god, but the idol was not literally the god. Thus, for example, a god, if angered, could leave the temple, but of course the statue of the god would remain. On the other hand, it was a very serious matter if a temple statue was damaged accidentally or destroyed by a conquering enemy; it was taken as a direct injury to or attack upon the person of the deity. We might say that, in some sense, the god resided "in" the image, and people took that presence very seriously. They placed garlands on statues of deities; dressed, washed, and fed them; and sacrificed and prayed to them. When New Testament authors used the single word "idolatry" as a term of opprobrium, they were condemning the whole of a vast multifaceted and subtle set of practices and beliefs.

The earliest Christians did not have temples, nor did they erect any imposing buildings. Believers met in a variety of existing and available places, which will be discussed when we turn to a closer treatment of cities. That ad hoc variety made for a very flexible organization and was probably an important factor in the growth of Christianity. Nevertheless, the idea of the temple was constantly in Christian minds, even though it might be immaterial—"a building from God, a house not made with hands, eternal in the heavens" (2 Cor. 5:1). Temple metaphors abounded in their writings. One obvious reason for this is that the temple is a recurring image in the Hebrew Bible, and New Testament authors were intimately acquainted with its descriptions. Gentile Christians, hearing the vivid words of 1 Peter 2:5 exhorting them to be as "stones built into a spiritual house, to be a holy priesthood, to offer spiritual sacrifices acceptable to God through Jesus Christ," could have drawn on their daily visual experience to furnish their imaginations. When Paul told the Corinthians (in 1 Cor. 3:16) that they were God's temple and that the Holy Spirit resided in their bodies, they would immediately have known what he was talking about. Christians saw gods living in temples every day, and non-Jewish believers had once believed that the buildings associated with them were suffused with divinity.

FESTIVALS

People were fiercely loyal to their cities, and hence proud of their temples and the fact that their gods lived there. Each city (and village) had a calendar of festive days dedicated to particular deities. The many ethnicities that made up the Roman Empire had their own sets of gods and practices that bound them to their geographical location and defined them as a particular group or people. In the Greek world there was no conception of a weekend—let alone a paid holiday—so when people did not have to work, festivals provided some irregular intermission from labor. They also helped people to celebrate the special relationship they had with the relevant god and functioned as an important means of socializing citizens into the fabric of city life and increasing their loyalty to their urban identity. Much of the free population of the city took part in the celebrations, which were, as one would expect, joyous and festive events. Processions of one kind or another played a major role in these events and might include the city magistrates and other leading citizens, priests, musicians, singers, dancers, acrobats, statues or painted images of the god, chariots, horses, incense, garlands, grain, baskets of fruit, and sweetmeats. They also included the animal or animals that were to be sacrificed to the god. In the city of Ephesus at the annual festival in honor of Artemis, the procession walked a circuit from her temple outside the city through the main street past all its major monuments, and back again. One report describes the way the procession included torches, baskets, incense, horses, dogs, and hunting weapons. Teenage girls also processed, to announce their readiness for marriage. They had their hair done up and wore special hunting costumes with quivers and arrows in imitation of Artemis, the virgin goddess of wild nature and hunting.[3] The procession concluded with the ritual sacrifice of an animal, or animal victims. A portion of meat was distributed to all the citizens in proportion to their social status. At the annual festival of Ephesian Artemis, there was also a distribution of money from the temple treasury.

When general or public misfortunes occurred, which might be attributed to divine anger, it was customary to offer sacrifices to win the favor of the god or to atone for past offences or oversights. Precisely the way this was imagined to work is a topic of considerable debate that lies outside the discussion here. What is important to observe is that in the ancient world, sacrifice was understood as a central means of communication with the divine world and a means of making requests, giving thanks, or seeking to repair a broken relationship with a deity. Indeed, the repair of broken relationships, whether between people and gods, offended parties, or cities, was marked with sacrifices that brought about reconciliation. Paul's language of reconciliation may reflect this political notion of sacrifice.

DAILY RITUALS AND RELIGIOUS EXPERTS

We have focused almost exclusively on temple rituals because these are so important to the beliefs and practices of emergent Christianity. However, people in antiquity practiced rituals of every imaginable kind. Many would be performed as matters of habit, with no more thought than we put into clinking glasses when having a drink, wishing someone luck, or kissing family members when we see them. Libation, for example, was a ritual that might be performed several times in a day. Before drinking wine (usually mixed with water), one poured a little out of the cup onto the ground in honor of Zeus and the Olympians, and when further cups were consumed, further libations attended them, moving down a set list of dedications. The hearth was the center of the Greek household and its goddess was Hestia, whose presence was signified by the presence of the hearth fire. Families started meals by offering a small libation of wine and a morsel of food on the hearth to honor Hestia. Roman domestic religion had analogous deities. Greeks and Romans were very fearful of the "evil eye"—a look which, maliciously or even involuntarily—could do them harm, as could an alarming variety of curses and spells. To protect themselves from such dangers, people wore amulets, especially of red coral, that took a variety of forms, such as erect phalluses, bells, and semiprecious stones with images of the gods or magical words on them. Some people protected their own private houses against malign forces and ill luck. The threshold might be guarded by Apollo Agyieus (of the Street) or Hercules, the latter usually represented by a schematic image of the club with which he defeated the Nemean Lion.

Greeks and Romans also had a repertoire of means to obtain messages from a god. Preeminent among them was to consult the oracle of Apollo at Delphi, where, if you were rich enough, you could go to hear from Apollo through his priestess what he might reveal concerning your future or a particular problem you were facing. The poor went to the local neighborhood oracle. People who thought they had an important dream went to experts in dream interpretation. Romans practiced augury, the reading of animal organs to learn of omens.

MAGIC

Finally, there was magic. As alluded to above, the practice of magic (and protection from it) was an important part of the

MAGIC = important

daily lives of the ancients. People in antiquity lived in a world utterly devoid of the kinds of social security and healthcare most of us in the First World today take for granted. Illness was a constant and present danger; many people were poor and undernourished; violence and injustice were pervasive. Their world was dominated by the idea of the "limited good"—what we now call a zero-sum game. There being only a limited quantity of good in the world (but unlimited evils), one person's gain must be someone else's loss. It is therefore hardly surprising that people felt very threatened by magic, curses, and spells, and thus set up innumerable apotropaic (i.e., protective) images, statuettes, altars, and figurines outside and within their houses to defend themselves. In Galatians 5:20, Paul, thinking of attempts to harm neighbors by means of spells, condemns "sorcery" right after idolatry. As might be expected in a milieu abounding in wishes both to project harm onto others and to avoid it oneself, there was a sort of service industry catering to those desires. Its practitioners were people—often polemically called magicians—whom we might regard as a set of religious entrepreneurs operating outside the civic systems of official religion. They claimed to have or were believed to possess extraordinary powers. In the New Testament a man named Simon is identified (again polemically) as a magician (Acts 8:9–24). (He is the Simon Magus of Christian legend.) On account of his amazing magical practices (v. 9), Samaritans identify him as "the power of God that is called Great" (v. 10). He has convinced them that a deity comes upon him and gives him power to perform wonders. Simon's story ends when, following his baptism, he offers money to Peter and John for the gift of the Holy Spirit through the laying on of hands (vv. 14–23). In a later Christian legend, in which things turn out badly for everybody, Simon's career continues in the court of Nero, where on account of his many wonders he convinces the emperor to worship him as a god. Simon's career comes to an abrupt end when the emperor summons

Peter and challenges the apostle to outperform Simon. The latter flies around the emperor's palace ceiling until Peter exorcises the demon holding him aloft and he plummets to his death, with the result that an outraged Nero orders Peter's execution.[4] Charges of magic could cut both ways, however. Celsus, a second-century opponent of Christianity, ridiculed the wonders of Jesus and those performed by his followers as deceptive acts performed by magicians.[5] In the ancient world, the antiquity of a religion assured its legitimacy. Accusing Jesus and his followers of magic was a means to denounce Christianity as evil or as a novel superstition.

DEMONS

People who made the transition from belief in many gods to early Christianity probably heard the claims of their new religion in essentially the same way that they had heard the claims of their pagan religion. New Testament writers, however, distanced themselves from the religions of their neighbors and urged their audiences to do the same. Christians, like Jews, associated belief in deities and the practices associated with them as inspired by malevolent powers, the devil/Satan, and demons. The authors of the New Testament probably took it for granted that their audiences had a mental framework into which the Christian message could be fitted, and so they did not provide a systematic treatment of these concepts. For example, Paul assumes the Corinthians will understand what he means when he advises them that to eat a meal in a temple is to sit at the table of demons (1 Cor. 10:14–21). Elsewhere, Paul speaks of believers once being slaves of evil, and he may have cosmic deities associated with natural phenomena or other lower gods in mind when he reminds the Galatians that they were once enslaved by *stoicheia tou kosmou* and *ta asthenē kai ptōcha stoicheia*

(Gal. 4.3, 9). Translating these phrases has been a challenge; the NRSV renders them as "elemental spirits of the universe" and "the weak and beggarly elemental spirits" in order to capture a notion of hostile cosmic powers. The phrase *stoicheia tou kosmou* appears in Colossians 2:8 (and again in Col. 1:20) and is probably related to "rulers and authorities" (2:15), as well as worship of angels (2:18). In 2:15 the death of Jesus is interpreted as a military triumph over them, thereby signifying their hostile power. The Letter to the Ephesians places believers in a battle "not against enemies of blood and flesh, but against the rulers, against the authorities, against the cosmic powers of this present darkness, against the spiritual forces of evil in the heavenly places" (Eph. 6:12). In Revelation, John calls Greek religion and its idols the "worshiping of demons" (Rev. 9:20).

Elsewhere, a host of other cosmic ideas drawn from ancient Near Eastern religion and passed on to early Christians through the Old Testament and other Jewish literature locate believers in a cosmic contest with evil. Angelology and demonology are central in this tradition. The angel Michael, for example, battles with the devil over the body of Moses after he dies (Jude 9). When war breaks out in heaven, Michael and his angels fight against "the dragon," and "that great serpent who is called the Devil and Satan, the deceiver of the whole world" is thrown down to earth and his angels with him (Rev. 12: 7–9). In Revelation "the Beast" is sent to a bottomless pit ruled by Abaddon/Apollyon (Greek and Hebrew for "the destroyer"; Rev. 9:11; 17:8). He rises from below the earth to compel the world to worship him (13:11–18) and returns there after God judges him (20:1, 3). In 2 Peter 2:4 he has been sent to the underworld, Tartarus (imprecisely rendered as "hell" in the NRSV)— the deepest region of Hades—which in the Greek world was where the wicked were sent for punishment. Jude 6 states, "The angels who did not keep their proper position, but left their proper dwelling, God has kept in eternal chains in the deepest darkness for the judgment of the great Day." 1 Peter 5:8 uses highly evocative language and draws from the popular practice of going to the arena to watch battles between humans and animals to warn them of their "adversary the devil" who is "like a roaring lion" that "prowls around, looking for someone to devour" (1 Pet. 5:8). James 4:7 exhorts, "Resist the devil, and he will flee from you." Here he is probably associating the devil with a Jewish idea of an evil impulse. These passages offer a collage of images not native (with the exception of Tartarus) to Greek religion. They transform a cosmos thick with divinities into one dense with demons.

EUCHARIST, BAPTISM, AND THE COSMOS

It is against this backdrop that New Testament references to the rituals of Eucharist and baptism take on a dramatic meaning. Indeed, they are cosmic events. We have already seen that Paul believes that the divine Christ is truly present in the meal Christians share and that improper conduct at the ritual can bring divine punishment. Further, as suggested above, Paul understands the meals Christians share are analogous to the meals held in association with blood sacrifice. Just as to partake of such pagan meals is to share in the power of demons, to partake of the Christ meal is to participate in the power of the risen Christ. The ritual of baptism also signifies cosmic realities even as it represents a dramatic and transformational event in the lives of Christians. Paul describes the status of people worshiping the gods as living under powers, under "the law of sin and death" (Rom. 8:2; 1 Cor. 15:26–28). These cosmic powers serve as divine agents to both humans and all of creation. By raising Christ from the dead, God has broken their power—those who were enslaved to them are now free to be the children of God they were created to be. In Romans 6:1–5 Paul talks about baptism as union with the death of Christ and a union with his resurrection. The baptized anticipate a full resurrection when Jesus returns to judge the world. However, they anticipate and live it even now through the Spirit who dwells in believers and is present at their meetings. Paul nowhere describes the precise ritual of baptism, but it probably included a dramatic attestation of the presence of the raised Spirit of Christ through ecstatic speech described in I Corinthians 14:4–39 or other signs. For example, newly baptized Christians may have called "Abba! Father!"—a title Jesus used to address God—to signify the presence of the raised Christ within them (Rom. 8:15; Gal. 4:6).

Colossians and Ephesians expand the cosmic aspects of this union with Christ's death and resurrection by emphasizing that Christ, having been raised from the dead, is seated beside God the Father and that every cosmic power is thus subject to him. First Peter 3:22 echoes this idea, interestingly in a context where baptism is discussed. Colossians 1:13 describes the death and resurrection of Christ as a rescue from the power of darkness and a transfer into the reign of God's son. And we have seen that Colossians also uses the military metaphor of a triumph to describe Christ's vanquishing of the cosmic powers (2:15). Baptism unites Christians with Christ's death and resurrection, which means that they now enjoy the benefits of Christ's defeat of and reign over the principalities and powers (2:9–13). They must not then worship cosmic powers or engage in other practices associated with them (2:16–23), because to do so is to "be taken captive" and return to the worship of the elements from which they have been rescued. Ephesians treats baptism as the creation of a new cosmic identity for Christians by enthroning them with Christ in the heavenly places "far above all rule and authority and power and dominion, and above every name that is named, not only in this age but also in the age to come" (Eph.

1:21; 2:6). Their victory has been achieved, but they neverthe-less continue in a cosmic battle "against the rulers, against the authorities, against the cosmic powers of this present darkness, against the spiritual forces of evil in the heavenly places" (6:12).

Baptism is a powerful ritual of cosmic ascent. It places Christians in a new space, above every other cosmic power, including those Greeks and Romans call gods. They no longer seek their benefaction, but they renounce it along with the powers they once worshiped.

QUESTIONS

We have considered a dramatic cosmology that rejected and swept aside the worship of the gods and the practices associ-ated with them. Nevertheless, however enthroned they were with Christ in the heavens, his believers still lived with both feet on the ground. There they were met with a host of chal-lenges that put them on a collision course with the society around them. In meeting those challenges they joined with Jews, who for centuries had wrestled with the best ways to live within a socio-religious order with beliefs and practices they often opposed. How were they to live in a world suffused with gift exchange rituals dedicated to the gods, on which the entire social order depended? What did they do now at fes-tivals? Did they no longer attend them? Did they take part while mentally rejecting the religious aspects of the celebra-tions, persuading themselves that that protected them from the charge of idolatry? Unlike their Jewish neighbors, Gentile believers had lived lives where multiple aspects of their daily life included rituals to deities. Did they stop conducting sac-rifices? If they did, what did their family members and neigh-bors think? We perhaps get a peek at what they thought from 1 Peter 4:4: "They are surprised that you no longer join them

in the same excesses of dissipation, and so they blaspheme."
Again, what if one partner, the wife, became a Christian and
her husband did not, as Paul describes in 1 Corinthians 7:13–
14? Did she stop performing the domestic rituals believed
to assure the security of the family? Did she let the hearth
fire go out as a sign that she no longer believed that Hestia
was protecting her household from harm? Did she refuse to
throw wine and food into the fire at the start of a meal? Did
Christians, when meeting friends at the tavern, not engage
in the set of ritual libations associated with drinking? What
if they got sick? Did they avoid going to temples where there
were rituals for healing? If they had a bad dream, did they
no longer go to dream interpreters? If they were perplexed
by a problem, did they still consult an oracle? Did they continue to wear amulets to protect them from curses and other
evils? Did they throw away their domestic gods, including
the ones that honored their ancestors? When they visited the
graves of loved ones, did they still pour libations of honey,
milk, oil, and wine to the dead and the chthonic deities? Did
they join with family members in commemorative meals at
the graveside, and did they still believe that the deceased was
present eating among them? The gods and their cosmos did
not go away when renounced by Christians. They were there
at every turn.

▼

THE EMPEROR AND

THE EMPIRE

> For the same reason you also pay taxes, for the authorities
> are God's servants, busy with this very thing. Pay all what is
> due them—taxes to whom taxes are due, revenue to whom
> revenue is due, respect for whom respect is due, honor to
> whom honor is due.
>
> —*Romans 13:6–7*

> Then I saw another beast that rose out of the earth; it had
> two horns like a lamb and it spoke like a dragon. It exercises
> all the authority of the first beast on its behalf, and it makes
> the earth and its inhabitants worship the first beast, whose
> mortal wound had been healed.
>
> —*Revelation 13:11–12*

ROMAN IMPERIAL FINGERPRINTS ARE ALL over the pages
of the New Testament. The names of cities, provinces, and emperors, as well as the references to specific events like Quirinius's
census in Luke's story of Jesus's birth (Luke 2:2) are the obvious
places we find them. A closer look reveals many more. We see
early Christians on Roman roads, plying trade, appealing to
imperial law, and describing the extremes of both the poverty
and the wealth of their contemporaries. This chapter turns from
consideration of the gods and the cosmos to a discussion of the
emperor and the empire. These should not be conceived of as

separate realms, however. Remember that there was no distinction between politics and religion in the world of the New Testament. Modern secular states separate religion and politics; in the ancient world they were inseparable. Thus, while much of this chapter takes up the "nuts and bolts" of imperial rule and administration, we should not lose sight of the importance of religion and ritual in the conduct of government. After discussing the historical, material, economic, and administrative aspects of Roman rule, the chapter concludes with a discussion of the role of the imperial cult and ritual as the primary means by which the emperor and his subjects communicated with each other. We will see the degree to which imperial realities and language suffused New Testament Christianity and the opportunities and challenges they presented for its adherents.

AVOIDING POPULAR MISCONCEPTIONS AND SIMPLISTIC JUDGMENTS

The emperor and the empire are not easily definable. The Roman Empire, like the United States, the United Kingdom, and the European Union, cannot be reduced to simplistic definitions or overly broad generalizations. The tens of millions of people ruled by Rome experienced and understood the empire differently and could expect different things from its social order. Likewise, the term "emperor" is a more complex designation for Rome's political leader than "prime minister," "president," or "chancellor" are for Great Britain, the United States, or Germany. First, the term did not mean the same thing everywhere in the empire. In the East, a living emperor could be worshiped as a god; in the West, such practice was generally restricted to posthumous worship. Second, in modern democracies a series of laws and institutional

structures restricts what political leaders can do and outlines bureaucratic procedures for achieving their aims. In the
case of the Roman Empire, the power, authority, and scope of
an emperor were much more elastic and evolved over time.
Finally, whereas titles like "prime minister" designate an office to which one is elected, "emperor" does not: it is not an
office, nor is it purely a function, but rather designates a kind
of power and authority specifically attached to a person. We
do not have an exact equivalent in modern political usage.
"Emperor" and "empire" are shorthand terms historians use
for the sake of convenience, but in doing so they know they
are referring to complex phenomena.

Varied portraits contrast with the way contemporary popular media and Christian imagination depict Rome and its
ruler. Those who rely on the modern media for their picture
of the Roman Empire (as in the 2000 film *Gladiator*) will usually come away with an incorrect understanding. In such in-

stances, entertainment trumps historical fact: the emperor is a
tyrant who practices debauchery by night and murder by day;
he believes he is a god and demands that people worship him.
His daily decisions have an immediate effect on the lives of the
millions of people he rules single-handedly. The people of the
Roman Empire, comprising mostly slaves, spend their few mis-
erable years making monuments and temples dedicated to the
worship of Rome's megalomaniac. The army is close at hand to
enforce worship of the emperor and brutally quash the slightest
threat of revolt. Christians, accordingly, keep an eye out for
ever-vigilant Roman authorities and spies, hastily scratch the
form of a fish in the sand to reveal their suppressed faith to one
another, and hide in catacombs when they are regularly hunted
down. In prison they write letters and give revelations craftily
coded to smuggle past Roman guards. Thousands die joyfully
singing hymns to Christ in the Roman Coliseum, where they
are fed to lions.

On the other hand, Hollywood's representation of Roman cruelty is tame at best, and it is telling that the empire's levels of poverty are never portrayed. Generally, we witness a middle-class Roman Empire that mirrors First World social realities. The movies that retell the story of the early church never place their narratives in the context of the abject poverty and urban filth that were typical of ancient cities. Viewing the tall and fit actors who have played Jesus, one would never guess that the historical Jesus, if he were typical of his day, was a short, more or less malnourished man with rotten and missing teeth, who was lucky to live into his thirties. When his crucifixion is depicted, Jesus remains stoic; he looks bloody but not brutalized by a gruesome execution. Mel Gibson's film *The Passion of the Christ*, for all its pornographic gore and anti-Semitism, comes closest to representing the degree of cruelty with which Rome treated its enemies and criminals. Even this picture, however, fails to convey what is unimaginable to us—that people might have come to watch such a death as a form of entertainment. There is nothing in our society to compare with the Roman pastime of going to the arena to watch animals and people die. A day's entertainment included seeing animals tear each other apart in the morning (the near extinction of certain large animals attests to the regularity and popularity of these spectacles), viewing criminals mauled by beasts over lunch, and then watching gladiators fight each other to the death in the afternoon.

Further, it is difficult for a First World person to understand the way all but the tiniest fraction of the empire's rural and urban population lived at or just above subsistence. The words of 1 Timothy 6:7 gain fresh meaning when read against this backdrop: "[W]e brought nothing into the world, so that we can take nothing out of it; but if we have food and clothing, we will be content with these." A new archaeological science of measuring first-century skeletal remains reveals differing levels of malnutrition and accounts for the high levels of mortality of the period due to susceptibility to sickness. With no understanding of germs and antibodies, doctors could do little to prevent infectious disease, nor could they combat it when it swept like wildfire through the cramped living quarters of a Roman city. The average life expectancy of a person born in the Roman Empire in the first century was roughly 23 years for a man and 25 years for a woman. The principal reason for these astonishingly low numbers is that more than half of all deaths occurred among children under 10, one-third of them before their first birthday. If one survived childhood, one's chances for a longer life improved, and one had a reasonable chance of living into one's early 50s. Nevertheless, only 5% lived beyond age 60.[1] Were we to be transported back to the first century, we would see a large number of young people and a noticeable absence of anyone over 55. Paul was not being abstract when he wrote of death's victory and sting (1 Cor. 15:55).

Finally, scholars often speak simplistically of New Testament authors being for or against the Roman Empire. When we consider this issue, we must be specific about what sense of empire we are using, what particular realities Christians may have supported or opposed, and how social location shaped their response to Rome. To put it differently, it is logically possible that both the passage from Romans and the one from Revelation of our epigraph can be true. It depends on what aspect of Rome Paul and John were thinking about when they wrote these things. Further, the Roman Empire affected people differently: women and slaves did not experience it in the same way that men, freedpersons, and citizens did. This fact is important when we remember that, according to Acts 22:25–29, Paul was not only male (as arguably most if not all of the rest of the authors of the New Testament were), but also a Roman citizen. The way gender and social status affect belief and practice becomes important when we recognize that New Testament writers adopted and adapted the metaphors and vocabulary of imperial political structures, the empire's ideals, and the emperor's rule to represent the lordship of Jesus and the hopes of their believers. For whom did these ideas resonate most strongly? Did all find them equally useful in describing their beliefs and expectations from their god? How might gender and social status have led them to hope for a revolutionary sweeping away of the political social order, or for an adjusted version of it? Rather than limiting our texts and their writers to simplistic binary oppositions of for and against, it is more fruitful to conceptualize Christianity in the Roman Empire as negotiated amid a dynamic set of social identities and practices.

"EMPIRE" AND "EMPEROR"

We have referred to the "Roman Empire" and the "emperor," which are terms that need explanation. As already stated, they are more complicated realities than we tend to realize, so to understand them we must consider social relations, cultural patterns, governing structures, geopolitical realities, rural and urban situations, and economics. In addition, our perception of the Roman Empire may be distorted by our perceptions of empires much closer to our time. The bureaucratic and ideological foundations of the European empires of Britain, France, Belgium, and Germany were modeled, at least in part, on what their leaders believed those of the Roman Empire to have been. We must therefore be attentive to the way in which our understandings of these later empires influence our vision of their mighty predecessor. Finally, we all live with the stereotypes of popular entertainment, and not just Hollywood sword and toga epics. The empire of the *Star Wars* films, for example, is a caricature of the Roman Empire combined with a pastiche of World War II German and British stereotypes. The films reveal the depth to which certain historical conceptions have penetrated the popular imagination. We risk arguing in a vicious circle if we allow these ideas to predetermine our thinking about the imperial world of the New Testament. Empire and emperor have meant differing things over the past two millennia.

What did "empire" and "emperor" mean in the first century? The words derive from the Latin terms *imperium* and *imperator*, both of which are based on the verb *imperare*, which means "to command." The meaning of these terms underwent a significant development in the closing decades of the first century BCE. Right up until the end of the Roman Republic—that is, prior to the reign of Augustus—*imperium* designated the power the state gave to a general to command an army for a specific battle, later a campaign, and for a limited time. The name *imperator* was an honorific title acclaimed by the troops to celebrate their general's victory over enemies. The term *imperium* also had a political meaning. It designated the power of an appointed official to exercise supreme authority in a legally defined jurisdiction for the benefit of the state.

Under Augustus these words gained new meanings. *Imperator* now meant one man, Augustus, holder of permanent power granted by the Senate to rule the entire Roman army—the vast legions stationed throughout the Mediterranean basin—and, going far beyond that, to rule entire provinces through proxy officials (legates, prefects, procurators) chosen by him and accountable directly to him. *Imperium*, for the first time, was used in a territorial sense to describe Rome's subject lands and peoples. Augustus claimed he governed the imperium on behalf of and for the benefit of the Republic; in reality, he inaugurated a monarchy. All the emperors from Tiberius onward would bear the titles of *imperator* and *Augustus* even as they were awarded titular offices (such as *pontifex maximus*, consul, and tribune of the people), each with its own powers. In the

Roman Empire, the passage of years was often expressed by reference to an emperor's regnal years. Luke cleverly plays with this by first marking Jesus's birth at the intersection of Augustus's reign and a census of Quirinius (Luke 2:1–2) and then representing Jesus's nativity in highly imperial terms (2:10–14). He thus declares that the baby in swaddling clothes in a manger is history's pivot, not Augustus.

A MEDITERRANEAN EMPIRE AND IMPERIAL NETWORKS

"And so we came to Rome" (Acts 28:14). The narrative arch of the Book of Acts ends on a climactic note when Paul reaches the imperial capital and preaches the Gospel. This action is, for its author, the fulfillment of Jesus's command given at the story's beginning, to be his "witnesses . . . to the ends of the earth" (Acts 1:8). By the time those words were written, "the ends of the earth" were distant indeed. Rome was a power ruling over an expanse of land that stretched thousands of kilometers from Britain and France in the west to the Tigris and Euphrates Rivers in the east, and from the Rhine and Danube Rivers in the north to the Sahara Desert in the south. A map (frontispiece) shows that the bulk of the empire was situated around the Mediterranean Sea, a fact that helped to bind dispersed peoples and cultures together and created the geographical conditions for rule by a single power. The Romans used a possessive pronoun to name the Mediterranean; they called it *mare nostrum,* "our sea."

As Rome's dominion expanded across the Mediterranean basin, it brought with it new laws, a universal currency, governing institutions, and colonial rule. Of course, it also brought the army and built a network of roads for it to march on—traces of which are seen today all over the map of Europe. The emperor could rule because of a cultural heritage bequeathed to him. Hellenism assured that Greek was widely spoken in cities in Greece, Asia Minor, the Levant, and eastern North Africa. This shared language assured that people separated by thousands of kilometers could read each other's writings. The authors of the New Testament and the Septuagint, as well as leading Jews like Philo and Josephus, all wrote in Greek. Latin, however, was the language of imperial administration and law. Roman colonies built on sites of conquered cities like Corinth, in the provinces, and on frontiers assured the penetration of Rome's culture across the empire's territories. Regular provincial censuses allowed for universal taxation and, in many areas, resulted in the transformation of barter economies into monetized ones. General freedom from war (at least in the areas where the New Testament writings we are considering came from) created a stable environment for commerce and trade. Growth in trade and population enabled small groups of entrepreneurs to raise themselves above subsistence. Paul traveled along trade routes, and he established new Christian communities where he did not find existing ones in the empire's chief trading centers: Antioch, Colossae, Ephesus, Philippi, Thessalonica, Corinth, and Rome. Each of the churches John's Revelation addresses (Ephesus, Smyrna, Pergamum, Thyatira, Sardis, Philadelphia, and Laodicea; Rev. 2–3) is in a city lying on a trade route. It is no accident that Christ believers in Acts are called "the Way" (Acts 9:2), a pun in Greek on the word for road. Roman roads brought together people who were otherwise separated by great distances and by differences of ethnicity, religion, and language. Acts adopts an imperial tone when it lists over fifteen different peoples living between Persia and Rome coming to Jerusalem at the church's first Pentecost and has them understand each other in their own tongues (Acts 2:9–11). This passage expresses an empire-wide imagination and the capacity to envision the world as a whole—an ability the Roman Empire helped shape.

The lands surrounding the Mediterranean are marked by great variations in climate and geography, but large areas with generally favorable conditions for agricultural production meant that an interconnected empire could withstand and compensate for anything but the worst disasters of famine, plague, and military invasion. The population, conservatively estimated in the first century at fifty to sixty million, underwent modest growth in this period. Roughly 80–90% of these people lived on the land and were engaged in agriculture; this fact contrasts with our world, where over half the global population lives in cities. That statistic can be misleading, however. Coastal regions were predictably more urbanized than the hinterland. On the west coast of Asia Minor (where many of Paul's letters were written), a much higher percentage of the population lived in cities. Ephesus, Pergamum, and possibly Smyrna (within a radius of 200 kilometers) each had a population of about 100,000, and thus were numbered among the megacities of the Roman Empire.

Of those who lived in cities, a very small fraction were aristocrats, elite officials, and large landholders (perhaps 1.5% of the urban population). The overwhelming majority was made up of the slaves, freedpersons, and freeborn poor who serviced them, along with the small-scale manufacturers and traders who produced goods for surrounding agricultural production. Being preindustrial cities, they were not organized to maximize industrial production and the creation of liquid capital as the modern city is, but rather as centers for elite consumption, religious practice, political rule, legal regulation, the collection of taxes, and a means of collecting and shipping items. The Book of Revelation is telling in this regard. In one of its visions, when merchants witness the destruction of Babylon (Rome), we hear them lament that "no one buys their cargo anymore, cargo of gold, silver, jewels and pearls, fine linen, purple, silk and scarlet, all kinds of scented wood, all articles of ivory, all articles of costly wood, bronze, iron, and marble, cinnamon, spice, incense, myrrh, frankincense, wine, olive oil, choice flour and wheat, cattle and sheep, horses and chariots, slaves—and human lives" (Rev. 18:11–13). Here the list of luxury goods, including slaves, speaks to elite urban consumption and economic disparity.

Alongside this cargo we should include shipments of foodstuffs to areas of the empire with lower levels of agricultural production because of differences in climate and quality of land. The existence of larger cities also required delivery of foodstuffs. In the case of western Asia Minor, with as many as 300,000 urban dwellers living within two hundred kilometers of each other, the means to meet the basic urban necessities far outstripped the resources of local farmers who were living at or just above subsistence. In Rome, where the population was perhaps as high as one million, the scale of the need was multiplied; the whole of Italy's agricultural production could not meet the demand.

RELIGIOUS TRAFFIC AND ENTREPRENEURS

An interconnected Mediterranean made imperial rule possible. Networks also offered a ready means for the spread of religious movements and set the context for the travels of the preachers and teachers who promoted them. Christianity was not the only belief system to benefit from this. Alongside it we can include, to name only a few better known examples, the cults of Mithras, Isis, Serapis, Dionysus, and, of course, the religion of Israel (as well as the spread of Stoic, Platonist, Cynic, Pythagorean, and other philosophical teachings). A networked Mediterranean also allowed migration from one tradition to another as different practices and ideas came into contact with each other.

The second-century satirist Lucian (ca. 120–ca. 180/200) presents a tale of one Peregrinus Proteus ("Shape Shifter Foreigner," after the god Proteus, whose form changes to avoid capture), who moves from one new cult to the next, taking advantage of their gullible believers along the way. His brief stop as a Christ worshiper lands him in jail, where he milks believers of their meager resources.[2] In another satire, Lucian tells the story of a charlatan religious entrepreneur, Alexander of Abonoteichus (ca. 105–ca. 170 CE), who concocted a snake-god, Glykon, as means of self-advancement; we watch Alexander travel from Pontus on the Black Sea to Rome, convincing people that he is an oracle of god and that he does wonders through his power.[3] Lucian uses both Peregrinus and Alexander to make fun of new religious movements and their promoters.

The Christianity of most of the New Testament developed in cities and their surrounding territories, some of which, like Rome, were populated by diverse peoples who brought with them their differing religious beliefs and cultural practices when they migrated there. Because of the importance of Judaism and Christianity in the development of Western culture, much scholarly attention has been directed to what we can know about their adherents. We know, for example, from surviving Jewish literature as well as archaeological evidence, that Jews had for centuries congregated in synagogues in Hellenistic cities, and that they learned to negotiate their religious and ethnic commitments in ways that made it possible for them to live within foreign cultural milieus and retain their identity. Alongside Jews, there were other similarly ethnically rooted religions that migrated into cities from other places. Like immigrant groups in general, they too will have struggled to preserve their various cultural identities and beliefs within a mosaic of cultures, and they will have found ways to adapt and accommodate themselves to new social realities.

The six to eight million Jews living in the imperial Diaspora did not all interpret and practice their religion in the same way. Unlike in later periods, Jews did not live in ghettoes, nor were they otherwise isolated from the rest of urban populations. There is a tendency among some New Testament scholars, in part relying on negative Roman descriptions, polemical Gospel representations of Pharisees, certain unrepresentative Jewish texts, and lingering stereotypes from centuries of European anti-Jewish prejudices, to emphasize the separation of Jews from society and to interpret Judaism as promoting a kind of religious-ethnic arrogance. In their view, Christianity, especially that advanced by Paul, is the antidote to Jewish misanthropy and works righteousness. The evidence, however, points to a much more complicated reality. For example, we know that the Jew Tiberius Julius Alexander was a provincial governor of Judea and Egypt under Claudius and Nero, respectively, and further that Jewish citizens served as city counselors, magistrates, and official envoys.[4] Under Augustus, inscriptions attest to Jews in Rome who enjoyed the emperor as their patron and honored him by calling themselves the *synagōgē tōn Augustēsiōn/ Augustōn*, the "synagogue of the Augustesions/Augustans." In some places, Jews were so integrated into urban society that, although we know they lived in certain cities, we glean virtually no information about them apart from inscriptions celebrating the civic offices and roles they enjoyed among their urban peers. But we also know that in places such as Alexandria and Rome, they were periodically the target of popular prejudice and suspicion. There is no single picture. The fact that Jews in the Diaspora spoke Greek, adapted their names to suit Roman and Greek usage, and used Greek political terms to describe their assemblies and leaders indicates an identity interwoven with larger political and cultural realities. The Roman policy, even after the rebellion of 66–74, was to tolerate and even protect Jewish religion and its practitioners.

It is a common misconception that the empire kept a close eye on diverse religious movements. Some argue that Christianity at first escaped imperial notice because it passed by unnoticed as a Jewish sect, and that because Judaism was a legally tolerated religion, Christians were first persecuted after they parted ways from their parent religion (traditionally dated to the last quarter of the first century). This traditional account has been called into question. Scholars are increasingly inclined to mark the separation of Judaism and Christianity as self-defined religions much later, in the fourth century. For the earlier period, as there was no normative Judaism or Christianity, the idea of "Christians" surviving unnoticed among "Jews" is unconvincing. More importantly, Rome had no ability, much less interest, in policing or closely scrutinizing these variegated religious beliefs or practices. Roman legal proceedings and justice were particularly brutal but not directed at any single religion in particular. The first time Christians were systematically targeted for their religious beliefs was under the emperors Diocletian (r. 284–305) and Galerius (r. 305–311) in a persecution from 303 to 311. There were periods of sporadic and local persecution before this time. However, when Christians were brought to their attention, Roman governors were motivated above all by a desire to preserve order. One sees this policy in action in Acts 18:12–16, when Paul in Corinth appears before the proconsul of Achaea, Gallio. The governor refuses to have him arrested, saying that he could only be persuaded to prosecute Paul if he were guilty of a serious crime. The second-century correspondence of Pliny the Younger, governor of Bithynia and Pontus, with the emperor Trajan, which asks for advice in cases where Christ believers are brought to his attention, reflects a similar policy. Pliny tortures and interrogates those denounced and imprisons believers who refuse to acknowledge the gods and the divinity of the emperor.[5] Misconceptions about the empire and its religions tempt us to think that this concern was caused by Christians refusing to worship the gods, especially the emperor.

But this idea is, in a sense, incorrect. It was not the rejection of emperor worship per se that concerned him, but rather the threat to civic order that he believed underlay it. To tolerate the rejection was to give up an element of control over the social and political order that he was responsible to maintain. Tellingly, Trajan also forbids people from denouncing Christians. Neither Trajan nor Pliny has any interest in seeking them out to prosecute them.

For some Christians it was a happy fact, even a sign of divine providence, that the rise of Christianity coincided with the creation of an empire that dominated the Mediterranean world. The third-century Christian theologian, biblical scholar, and philosopher Origen celebrated the rise of Rome and the spread of the Christian Gospel as a divinely ordained two-stage process for preaching the Gospel to the world. In other words, God had arranged the birth of Jesus to coincide with the rise of Augustus and his establishment of the *Pax Romana* in order to allow an empire-wide expansion of the rule of Christ and his church. Caesar brought an order based on military force, and Christ brought a superseding order based on God's love through the church's preaching of his Gospel throughout the world.[6] Others, such as the author of the Book of the Revelation, took a more sinister view. If Rome's dominance and the Gospel's message signified anything, it was a cosmic war between irreconcilable powers. John's final invitation to come to drink from the water of life flowing through the heavenly Jerusalem as *a gift* (Rev. 22:17) sharply contrasts the rapacious violence and greed of the imperial authorities and merchants John describes in Revelation 17–18. Origen's point of view, however, was also derived from the New Testament: in Romans 13:1–7, Paul urges Christ followers to submit to the emperor and pay their taxes; 1 Peter 2:13–14 exhorts them likewise; and 1 Timothy 2:1–2 instructs "supplications, prayers and intercessions, and thanksgiving be made for everyone, for emperors and all who are in high positions, so that we may lead a quiet and peaceable life in all godliness and dignity" (1 Tim. 2:1–2, NRSV slightly altered). Jesus's command in Matthew 22:21 to pay Caesar what is Caesar's and God what is God's is interpreted in the New Testament, as it has been ever since, in widely differing ways.

PROVINCIAL ADMINISTRATION, TAXES, LITURGIES, AND HONORS

For a dominion that stretched thousands of kilometers and exercised control over some forty-five million people under Augustus and sixty million by the middle of the second century, the Roman imperial government had a surprisingly thin bureaucracy. The Book of Acts, as well as the Gospels, introduces us to the empire's chief provincial bureaucrats, the legate and the proconsul. There were more, of course, but even so there were perhaps only 360 Roman officials occupying posts in any given year during the Augustan period. The empire's administrative structures were directed to two simple goals: the preservation of order and the successful collection of taxes. Some historians distinguish between conquest empires and tribute empires. Conquest empires roll over territories like a tsunami; they expand quickly but are subject to rapid collapse unless they develop institutions for prolonged government. Tribute empires have a longer life because they build institutions and structures for the stable administration of conquered territories. Whereas the Republican Empire was a conquest empire, Augustus's achievement was to turn it into a tribute empire, as attested by its building of roads, uses of diplomacy, and establishment of institutions for the administration of law. In the case of tax collection, for example, the Romans relied, so far as possible, on the systems that existed before their arrival. Hellenistic empires of the Greek East had developed the means for its resident elites to govern those in the countryside and extract wealth from their land through taxes and rents. The empire simply adapted preexisting institutions to assure that a measure of the wealth extracted by cities came to Rome in the form of tribute.

Contrary to popular opinion, the Roman Empire was not a police state. Rome had an army of 250,000 soldiers, half of whom were provincial conscripts, and most of whom were deployed along the Rhine-Danube frontier to protect the empire from incursions by differing tribes of people. With this perpetual menace in the north, and 6.5 million square kilometers (2.5 million square miles) of empire to control, the emperor could hardly spare soldiers to stand at every corner waiting to snatch Christ followers.

In the first century there were roughly forty provinces divided into two groups, "senatorial" and "imperial." The Senate governed one set through proconsuls selected by lot. The emperor directly ruled the second set through governors (legates) he personally chose. For larger provinces, he appointed legates selected from the body of former consuls and praetors. The New Testament names Quirinius as legate of Syria (Luke 2:2); he was appointed by Augustus in 6 CE. For smaller, as well as troubled, provinces, he appointed equestrians (lower Roman magistrates) to govern as legates, again responsible only to him. In addition to these legates were the commanders of legions ("legionary legates"), who might be senators or equestrians, and who used the army to subjugate any unruly provincial population. The New Testament's most famous legate is Pontius Pilate, appointed to administer Judea. Roman Judea was an administrative satellite of Syria, and Pilate was under the authority of its proconsul. The legate or proconsul took with him a junior senator called a quaestor, who was assigned financial responsibilities as well as a body of friends to advise him, and slaves and freedmen to function as minor officials. The emperor also had at his disposal the imperial household (*familia Caesaris*), a vast body of slaves and freedpersons who performed routine administrative tasks in Rome and in all the provinces, mainly concerned with taxation, legal meetings and petitions, and running the increasingly numerous imperial estates. When Paul sends greetings to the Philippians from "the emperor's household" (Phil. 4:22), he is referring to Christians who are probably slaves or freedpersons in the imperial administration.

A provincial governor's chief tasks were to dispense justice; assure that public works such as roads, aqueducts, and temples were being properly maintained; and assure the collection of taxes (the *tributum*) to Rome. To fulfill his legal responsibilities, the governor heard cases and traveled a circuit (*conventus*) to adjudicate more serious cases. Tax collection was focused on the empire's *peregrini* (literally "foreigners," "ones from abroad"), a Latin term that refers to non-Roman people, who constituted roughly 90% of the population. The result was the systematic extraction of wealth from every corner of the empire, with the exception of the residents of Italy, who, alongside Roman citizens, were not taxed. Romans collected an annual head tax plus a tax on goods, together amounting to 10–20% of total income, depending on where in the empire one lived. From a modern perspective, where income taxes average 32%, this seems low, but for those living at or just above subsistence the rate could be devastating. Additionally, tenant farmers also paid rents in cash or in kind to landowners, and most city dwellers rented rooms. The majority of urban merchants paid rent for the shops where they conducted their businesses. There were also customs taxes on shipped goods of up to 25% at provincial and other boundaries. At times there were supplementary taxes, such as when requisitions were needed for the army. In addition, locals were at the mercy of tax farmers, who bid against one another for contracts to collect taxes on behalf of civic officials, a practice that led to the extortion of the population. Taken together, this resulted in an economic system of merciless exploitation.

The total tribute owing from each tax area was established by the amount of land divided by the population multiplied by the tax rate. Tribute was always assessed through a census; Luke 2:2 describes a census of Galilee and Judea conducted by the legate Quirinius. The governor depended on local civic officials for collecting tribute, which was an immense burden for them, but they had a vested interest in cooperating with governors, because cooperation guaranteed their social position. Payment was in cash or in kind; in-kind payments would be sold by collecting agents to get the cash required for the tribute payment. The city made up for any shortfall. The tribute required a standardized means of economic measurement, which was provided by Roman coinage issued from official mints. An imperially appointed quaestor, who had the authority to audit tax records, assured that local officials were paying the amount of taxes the population owed.

A general feature of the governance of eastern Mediterranean cities was evergetism, a continuing relationship of gift-giving in return for honors that bound the elites (patrons) and their beneficiaries (clients). The empire may be imagined as a complex and sophisticated network of patrons and clients centered in the practices of gift exchange. Its aristocrats and wealthy citizens governed cities. These were usually men, but as the first century progressed, government in a few instances included women who held land in their own names, priesthoods, and other civic offices. Unlike today, higher officials were not paid; election to office was rather an honor in return for which incumbents were expected to act as patrons and to furnish city residents with benefits. These benefits, called liturgies, took the form of donation of funds for things like the celebration of religious festivals (usually including processions, games, sacrifices, and distributions of food), as well as the construction of buildings, public works, and monuments. Liturgies were a form of conspicuous display of wealth and the means of gaining and advertising status. Those with wealth were expected to engage in this kind of gift-giving, and we see some of the rich trying to dodge this responsibility by refusing elected office. The liturgical system accorded elites a degree of sovereignty over urban affairs, although the first-century philosopher Plutarch quipped that a local official should never forget how close the Roman boots of legionaries were to his neck.

Generous performance of a liturgy won a patron honor from his or her clients and resulted in further patronage, thus perpetuating the culture of gift exchange discussed earlier with respect to the gods and their worshipers. Statues of benefactors and inscriptions heralding their virtues and boasting of benefactions were a chief means of honoring civic elites. Of course, the liturgical system concealed the fact that the wealthy could only give benefits by exploiting the populations to which they offered benefactions. They were giving people a small percentage of what they took from them. The Book of James offers a pointed critique: "Listen! The wages of the laborers who mowed your fields, which you kept back by fraud, cry out, and the cries of the harvesters have reached the ears of the Lord of hosts. You have lived on the earth in luxury and in pleasure; you have fattened your hearts in a day of slaughter. You have condemned and murdered the righteous one, who does not resist you" (James 5:4–6). On a larger scale, the elite populations of the empire also looked to the emperor for largesse, which similarly took the form of funding festivals, games and distributions, monuments, and the building of structures like aqueducts.

CHRIST OR CAESAR?

One of the most widely known facts about the Roman Empire is that people worshiped the emperor as a god. Unfortunately, often connected with this knowledge is the popular misconception that the emperor must therefore have been a megalomaniac and that he executed people who refused to worship him. While there is evidence to support the egomania of some emperors, chief among them Gaius (Caligula) and Domitian, there is nothing to suggest that people were executed because they did not worship the emperor. It is true that people could be required to prove their allegiance to the emperor by honoring him as a deity (as when Pliny required Christians to honor Trajan). However, this was not so much motivated by pathology as it was by a need to have subjects recognize the divine power that brought the emperor his *imperium* and enabled him to govern well. Again, religion and politics were inseparable. Also suffering from a good deal of misconception is the way a good deal of New Testament scholarship portrays the imperial cult. Some scholars have argued that there was a single imperial cult and that it was the glue that held the Roman Empire together, but neither of these claims is true. First, the empire at its manifold levels was held together through the complex series of mechanisms discussed above, of which one element among many was emperor worship. Second, there was no singular imperial cult. There were rather varieties of emperor worship that reflected local initiatives and traditions and that changed from one emperor to the next.

The cult offered to emperors in the West was different from that practiced in the Greek East, where there was a long tradition of worshiping rulers and generals as gods, and living emperors were worshiped as divine. In the West, Rome's emperors were deified by an act of the Senate *after* death. Cult was a form of honor not to the emperor per se, but to the divine power he must have possessed to allow him to achieve extraordinary things. Figure 3.1, from a frieze of an imperial temple in Ephesus, shows a representation of the posthumous apotheosis of Lucius Verus (130–69 CE), honored by the Senate with divination on account of his military victories.

FIGURE 3.1 Relief of the apotheosis of Lucius Verus, Ephesus, second century CE. The emperor on a chariot, accompanied by a winged victory, rises heavenward. Virtus, signifying the emperor's divine virtues and prowess, leads the chariot with Helios (the sun god) standing behind him. Below is Tellus, goddess of earthy abundance and fertility, signified by a cornucopia and a child. The relief captures the earthly benefits of the emperor's rule as well as his virtues as the reasons for his apotheosis. Photo by author. Kunsthistorisches Museum, Vienna.

This was the normal path to worship as a divinity. The emperor Gaius caused a public scandal when he transgressed tradition and pretended he was a god when still alive, and Nero broke with custom when he had coins made depicting him with a radiate crown, a symbol of divinity and an iconographical representation reserved for posthumous representation. The successor of an emperor was interested in assuring his father was deified, as this act allowed him to designate himself with the honorific title *divi filius*, son of god, a testimony that he too possessed a personal divine power to do great things. Nero, for example, after his accession, worked hard to have his adoptive father, Claudius, deified. The philosopher Seneca (4–65 CE) wrote a satire called *The Pumpkinification of Claudius*, in which the gods debate whether to admit the inept emperor into their company following the vote by the Senate to deify him. The emperor Vespasian's dying words were rumored to have been, "Oh dear, I think I'm becoming a god."[8]

The importance of the imperial cult does not lie in its revelation of imperial pathology but in what it teaches us about the way rituals of gift exchange and honors was an important means by which ruler and ruled communicated with each other for their mutual benefit. This can be seen, first, by the fact that the emperor did not demand worship but rather received petitions to be granted a privilege of worshiping him; the permission to offer cult was awarded by the Senate. Local elites, a community, or a group of cities could make application to host an imperial cult in their city or area, but they were not always successful. Second, requests for special favors usually accompanied these petitions. The offering of emperor worship was thus a means of communication between the emperor and his subjects, a way of building relationships with political powers and, through proof of loyalty, a means of gleaning certain benefits. Third, one should not conclude from this that the imperial cult was solely a way to manipulate the emperor or vice versa; that is, that emperor worship could be reduced to a shrewd form of politics. The material evidence shows that we must understand worship of the emperor in the same light that we view Greek and Roman religion. The gods were accessible through right ritual, and one expected certain gifts by honoring them correctly. The emperor as a divinity was a similar case. We are inclined to ask whether people really believed the emperor was a god. The evidence indicates they did: they prayed to him, they honored his statue as though he were personally present, and so on. But the question already presumes a Christian way of approaching the issue. What people believed was that ritual was an effective means of communicating with the gods. They practiced ritual to make requests, secure certain benefits, and guarantee the continuation of those already received.

The warrant for offering cult to a living emperor was found in the benefits his rule brought. In one important inscription dating from 9 BCE found at the city of Priene on the west coast of Asia Minor, an assembly of cities decrees worship of Augustus on September 23, his birthday, because divine providence arranged his birth to mark the beginning of good news for the world; namely, the end of civil war and the reestablishment of political order. The decree reads, in part, as follows:

> Decree of the Greek Assembly in the province of Asia, on motion of the High Priest Apolionios, son of Menophilos, of Aizanoi: whereas Providence that orders all our lives has in her display of concern and generosity in our behalf adorned our lives with the highest good: Augustus, whom she has filled with virtue [arētē] for the benefit of humanity, and has in her beneficence granted us and those who will come after us a Savior [sōtēr] who has made war to cease and who shall put everything in peaceful order; and whereas Caesar, when he was manifest [epiphaneis], transcended the expectations of all who had anticipated the good news, not only by surpassing the benefits conferred by his predecessors but by leaving no expectation of surpassing him to those who would come after him, with the result that the birthday of our God signalled the beginning of Good News [euangelion] for the world because of him; . . . proconsul Paul Fabius Maximus has discovered a way to honour Augustus that was hitherto unknown among the Greeks, namely to reckon time from the date of his nativity; therefore, with the blessings of Good Fortune and for their own welfare, the Greeks in Asia Decreed that the New Year begin for all the cities on September 23, which is the birthday of Augustus; and, to ensure that the dates coincide in every city, all documents are to carry both the Roman and the Greek date, and the first month shall, in accordance with the decree, be

observed as the Month of Caesar, beginning with 23 September, the birthday of Caesar.[9]

The decree states that the emperor is to be worshiped because providence filled him with virtue that benefited the world. It goes on to describe him as "a savior" who ended war and will put everything in order. It describes his birth as an epiphany. It is notable that the inscription states divine providence fills Augustus with virtue for the benefaction of the world. It contains a surprising number of words that appear in the New Testament to describe the reign of Christ.

As political language, the decree offers us a view of imperial ideology. The Romans promoted the view that the gods had placed them as supreme rulers of the world because they were especially virtuous (hence the reference to Augustus's *arête*). The poet Virgil has Jupiter acclaim, "To the Romans I assign no limit of things nor of time. To them I have given empire without end" (*Aeneid* 1.278). He also has Anchises, the father of Aeneas (the heroic patriarch of the Roman people), tell his son, "Roman, remember by your strength to rule / Earth's peoples—for your arts are to be these: / To pacify, to impose the rule of law, / To spare the conquered, battle down the proud" (6.1151–1154). Virgil here promotes an Augustan ideology that explains the reasons Rome should govern: because of its might, its power to pacify, and to practice justice. Further, he outlines a global vision: it is the earth's peoples who are to receive Rome's arts of war and diplomacy. An empire without end is Jupiter's gift to the Romans; the emperor as his vice-regent rules the earth.

While Virgil depicts the Romans as sparing the conquered, they often governed conquered nations with brutal force. At an imperial cult temple at Aphrodisias in Asia Minor, one finds a row of female statues, each personifying a different nation conquered by Augustus. Above them one sees depictions of the

emperor, often in military dress, in the company of the gods
or depicted as one of them. This is the image of the peoples
of the world brought into unity under the divinely appointed
emperor who achieves magnificent things through divine
power. This was the way Rome articulated the idea of universal

FIGURE 3.2 Relief of Claudius's victory in Britannia, Aphrodisias, first
century CE. Photo by author. Aphrodisias Museum, Aphrodisias, Turkey.

humankind that was first conceptualized in the Hellenistic period. We also witness a violent gender politics: the victor is male and the vanquished is female. Some of the images in the upper register imply the emperor's rape of women as a sign of potency and supremacy, as can be seen in Figure 3.2, where Claudius is represented conquering Britannia, personified as a subjugated woman, in celebration of his victories in Britain and its subsequent absorption into the Empire.

These images were deemed sufficient to their purpose as they stood. They did not require some equivalent to an instruction manual to explain how the divine and the human could coexist in the person of the emperor. Christians, on the other hand, would spend over six centuries debating the union of the divine and human natures in Jesus of Nazareth. Such debate was not an issue in the imperial cult because the interest was in benefactions and honors rather than metaphysics.

We have noted that the Priene inscription contains a number of words that the New Testament uses to describe the reign of Christ. For example, it calls the birth of Augustus "the beginning of good tidings [*euangelion*]," and the "appearing [*epiphanein*]" of a "savior [*sōtēr*]" and his rule as bringing an end to war and peace (*eirēnē*). *Euangelion* can also be translated as "gospel," a word (together with cognates) found 133 times in the New Testament. Such language also appears regularly on coins and other inscriptions to describe the emperor as "son of god" (*huios theou*), "lord" (*kyrios*), and a "mediator" (*mesitēs*); his reign is described as "salvation" (*sōtēria*), and his birth or an imperial visit as an arrival (*parousia*). Ephesians 2:17 after a reference to Jesus's death and resurrection as bringing reconciliation and bringing hostility to end (v. 16), states that Christ "came and proclaimed good news [*euēngelisato*] of peace [*eirēnē*] to those who were far off (i.e., Gentiles) and those who were near (Jews)" (NRSV, slightly altered). Here themes of hostility, peace, and the unity of peoples come together not through Caesar but through Christ.

Many scholars, noting the parallels of these terms in New Testament descriptions of Jesus, have argued that early Christians used imperial language to honor Christ in order to polemicize against emperor worship. This is true in some instances, as we can see in the Book of Revelation. Revelation exalts Jesus by using panegyric language we know was used to acclaim the emperor imperial (5:13). The whole of Revelation 13 is an extended polemic against the Beast and his minions, immediately followed by chapter 14, an extended panegyric to the Lamb who will come to vanquish the Beast, the emperor, who demanded that people worship him (13:1–18)—a clear reference to the imperial cult in Asia Minor. However, alongside polemic, New Testament authors were motivated to use language that expressed the universal claims they made for Jesus. From the Hellenistic era onward, and then in the Roman period, a series of terms like the ones listed above appeared repeatedly to communicate the divinely arranged geopolitical benefits of a particular ruler's reign. The terms were often associated with images found on coins, monuments, reliefs, statues, and placards. The empire's cities were saturated with such imagery. Imperial images furnished a ready means for New Testament writers and their audiences to portray and imagine the scope and benefits of Christ's achievements and reign.

Once we are attentive to it, we discover political language in many of the universal assertions of New Testament authors. For example in Colossians 1:6, Paul describes the Gospel as "bearing fruit and growing in the whole world." Later, he describes the death of Christ as "making peace" (1:20) and bringing reconciliation (1:20, 22), or as a "triumph" over cosmic powers (2:15). He also states that because of Christ's rule there are no longer "Jews and Greeks, circumcised and uncircumcised, barbarian, Scythian, slave and free, for Christ is all and in all" (Col. 3–11). These are terms that resonate with imperial associations. Peace and triumph invoke military metaphors of pacification and conquest, and reconciliation speaks to the end of political hostility through a peace treaty. The reference to Scythians invokes the claims of the Roman Empire to govern the world. However, unlike Caesar's dominion, which stopped at the border of Scythia (an area surrounding the north coast of the Black Sea), Christ's dominion extends to include the Scythians and, by implication, all peoples beyond them. In other words, there is no region Christ's reign cannot penetrate and no obstacle to its peace and reconciliation. Its Gospel is growing not only in the Roman Empire, but also outside it to embrace the whole world.

New Testament authors also draw on imperial language when they describe themselves as engaged in a battle, "not against enemies of blood and flesh, but against the rulers, against the authorities, against the cosmic powers of this present darkness, against the spiritual forces of evil in the heavenly places" (Eph. 6:12). Similarly we see it when they exhort believers "to take up the whole armor of God," and then go on to use vivid images of putting on a breastplate, helmet, and wielding sword and shield to describe the hope, faith, righteousness, salvation, and peace they are to possess (Eph. 6:13–17; also, 1 Thess. 5:8). An imperial tone of conquest appears as well in the representation of the enthronement of Christ and the universal acclamation of the lordship of Christ (Phil. 2:11). When Christians heard the author of Hebrews use the description of Psalms 110:1, which describes vanquished enemies as the footstool for the Lord's anointed, to portray Christ's exaltation and seat at the right hand of God (Heb. 1:13), they could have envisioned imperial iconography. Commonplace in this imagery were portraits of emperors standing over seated and bound captives. The ultimate version of an application of imperial imagery appears in the Book of Revelation, where Jesus vanquishes his enemies. There we see him on a white horse, slaying with a sword from his mouth and covered in blood (Rev. 19:11–16). This portrayal was not without paradox, since in the Apocalypse Jesus conquers by his death (Rev. 12:10–11)—the blood covering his cloak in 19:13 is his own! And in Colossians 2:15, Jesus's triumph occurs on the cross. Of course, one also finds language of conquest, royal rule, putting on armor, pacification of enemies, and so on in the Hebrew Bible, and it is clear to us that Israel's Scriptures provided an important source of such imagery for New Testament writers. The point here is that when it was invoked before an audience of non-Jewish Christians, unaware of Hebrew texts but primed by the picture language of Roman rule, they would turn to what they knew to form a mental picture of what such imagery described.

We can expect that these kinds of claims and confessions were received differently depending on the receiver's status, gender, and economic location. The Apocalypse can be read—as most of us have been taught to read it—as a book of comfort and promise to those victimized by Roman imperial ideology. However, one can also read it as a frightening assault on those Christians too comfortable within the imperial order. It is possible to interpret its representation of Christ as the ruler truly worthy of the imperial acclamations in the heavenly throne room of Revelation 5:12–14 as a stern warning to those who are enjoying the material rewards of the empire. For example, the sustained diatribe against the Laodiceans of Revelation 3:15–22 tells those who think they are rich and need nothing that what they really are is "wretched, pitiable, poor, blind, and naked." Reading that would surely raise qualms in some Christians beyond the borders of Laodicea.

These observations raise, again, the question of the function of such language in creating identity, and they ask us to consider when, how, and in what situations imperial terms and acclamations were most salient. It seems clear that the Book of Revelation wants to establish relevance to the mundane world of economics and commerce, hence its vivid presentations of the dirges of merchants, shipmasters, seafarers, and sailors who mourn Babylon's (Rome) destruction (Rev. 18:9–19). Perhaps it is warning Christians who are urban manufacturers working in their shops or merchants who enjoy a degree of prosperity under a successful imperial administration that they are living in an idolatrous regime destined for destruction, and that they must therefore separate themselves from the empire. The advice to be subject to imperial rulers and to pay taxes in Romans 13:1–7, and to pray and even give thanks for rulers in 1 Timothy 2:1–2, suggests the nurturing of a different kind of identity, as does the similar exhortation in 1 Peter 2:13–14. The Book of Revelation, with its pictures of social chaos and war, emphasizes the way Satan uses the emperor to wreak havoc and disorder in the world, while the passages in Romans and 1 Peter make the contradictory point that God uses the emperor to bring and preserve order. Finally, we may ask, when New Testament authors use a political term, "gospel" (*euangelion*), to describe the message of the death and resurrection of Christ, what sort of picture would differing audiences of his letters have taken away? Would they have imagined with Origen that Christ and Caesar were working together to create a new order? Or would they have taken John's view that Christ was coming to overthrow the emperor? If they believed the latter, when was such belief most relevant? Did it become determinative at an imperial festival, the games the emperor hosted, the distributions of food that were part of celebrating Rome's ruler as divine, in Christ worship, before a governor like Pliny or Gallio, at the market place, or at the arena? Did Christian belief come to mind when believers paid taxes, when commanding a slave or receiving orders from a master, when obeying a husband, or when taking advantage in a new climate for women to enjoy new forms of economic power and status? The gospels of Christ and of Caesar could mean a host of things in varying contexts and at different times.

THE CITY AND ITS

RESIDENTS

Erastus, the city treasurer, and our brother Quartus,
greet you.

—*Romans 16:23*

For here we have no lasting city, but we are looking for the
city that is to come.

—*Hebrews 13:14*

THE GOSPELS ARE RURAL STORIES. Jesus wanders the Galilean
countryside, largely avoiding towns and cities, and teaches
with metaphors and stories at home in the world of peasant
farmers. Once past Matthew, Mark, Luke, and John, however,
the New Testament takes a sharp turn for the city. The story
that Acts tells of the expansion of Christianity is an urban tale
with a focus on Paul and his travels from city to city around the
Mediterranean basin. Its canonical location after the Gospels
and before the Pauline Epistles sets the stage for the letters to
differing city assemblies of Christians that follow. The New
Testament ends with a vision of a city, the New Jerusalem, de-
scending from heaven to earth (Rev. 21:2). Since only 10–20%
of the population of the Mediterranean world lived in cities,
the urban dimensions of the New Testament reflect the life-
worlds of a small, numerically unrepresentative, yet culturally
dominant Greek-speaking audience. Further, urban dwellers

were not preoccupied with the rural realities of Jesus's Galilean world. It is most likely that the audiences of the greater part of the New Testament were artisans, unskilled city workers, urban slaves, and free persons, not farmers. The shift from country to city required a good deal of translation of Jesus's teaching and of the meaning of his death and resurrection to make sense in a new setting. The goal of this chapter is to offer a portrait of the first-century urban world in which Christians lived in order to furnish a basic understanding of the conditions under which that translation took place.

The challenges of city living were different from those in the countryside. Chief among these was urban poverty. One possible reason for successful recruitment to Christianity was Jesus's message of welcoming and caring for outsiders, in this case the urban poor. As his teachings and the meaning of his death and resurrection found new meanings among this social group, they also created an opportunity for reconstructing the way imperial urban life was to be practiced and understood. Further, as Christian belief and practice took root in a new cosmopolitan audience of Diaspora Jews, diverse ethnicities, and worshipers of Greco-Roman and local deities, believers had to find a language for folding varying beliefs, rituals, and social interests into a unifying vision. Against this backdrop, both Paul's celebration of baptism as removing traditional lines of demarcation between Jew and Greek, slave and free, male and female (Gal. 3:28), and the Pauline affirmation of Christ breaking down dividing walls of religious hostility (Eph. 2:14) promoted cohesion.

Paul's inclusive statement may also reflect the cultural diversity of the imperial urban world. The first-century cities where Christianity grew were discovering a new cosmopolitanism through the travel, migration, economic opportunities, and interreligious encounter the Roman Empire made possible. Christianity, networked across cities and linking a variety of social groups and erstwhile followers of differing religions, is symptomatic of new forms of urban contact that were taking place across the empire. As it strategically inserted itself into city life and brought new opportunities for advancement, Christianity helped to connect dispersed city assemblies and diverse peoples, religions, languages, and customs into a new overarching social and religious order. For all of its language of separation from an idolatrous world, the New Testament in fact attests to participation in a larger urban phenomenon taking place across the empire.

Perhaps more important than belief was practice. The teaching of 1 John 4:20–21 takes on a particular meaning it may not nowadays have among suburban First World believers often shielded from differences of demography, religion, and economic status: "Those who say, 'I love God,' and hate their brothers or sisters, are liars; for those who do not love a brother or sister whom they have seen, cannot love God whom they have not seen." A message that taught the responsibilities believers had to one another to transcend social boundaries and offer one another welcome and support resulted in a transformation of the urban Mediterranean and ultimately the Roman Empire itself.

A NETWORK OF CITIES

As Rome expanded its dominion across the Mediterranean world, it transformed cities and their surrounding populations. Although only 10–20% of people lived in cities and towns (the vast majority of them with less than five thousand inhabitants), their importance far outweighed their numbers. It was through those cities and towns that Rome delivered imperial administration and political control. Cities that had functioned as autonomous states in the Hellenistic period now belonged to a trans-urban Roman political, administrative, and economic network. The New Testament itself is a testament to this reality. Letters written and carried from one Christian assembly to another hundreds or even thousands of kilometers away are symptomatic of empire-wide interurban communication and travel. A map of the roads connecting the cities of Asia Minor and Greece named in the New Testament (Figure 4.1) reveals the importance of urban networks for the growth of a new religious movement.

First, it shows that early Christian assemblies were located in cities at junctions of Roman roads. Second, it indicates how close they were to one another. Laodicea, Colossae, and Hierapolis are less than a day's walk away from each other. Each of the seven churches addressed by Revelation (2:1—3:22) lies on a major trade route and is relatively close to the others. Ephesus, Smyrna, and Pergamum are at or near the coast; Ephesus and Smyrna, as well as Pergamum, Thyatira, Sardis, and Philadelphia, are a two day's walking journey from each other; Laodicea is a four-day journey from Philadelphia and five days from Ephesus. In the same manner, Philippi, Thessalonica, and Beroea are in close proximity and lie on the Via Egnatia, a main overland route for the transportation of goods from east to west. Corinth and Cenchreae, a few kilometers apart, were located on either side of an isthmus crossed by a slipway for ships that facilitated the shipment of goods from the eastern to the western Mediterranean.

All of these cities were parts of an imperial system in which the provinces were carved into territories administered from major urban centers. Proximity also inevitably resulted both in minor territorial disputes and in competition for status in the eyes of the emperor. To resolve conflicts, city leaders appealed to overarching values that transcended interurban differences and competition—values such as belonging to a single human race, sharing a common cultural heritage, or being descended

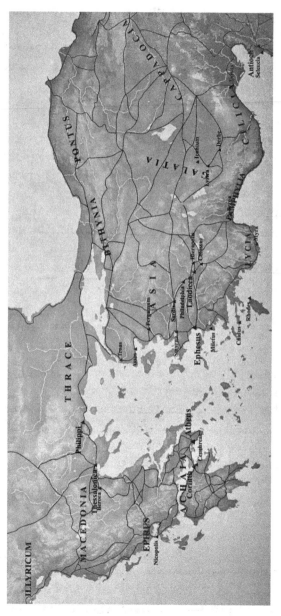

FIGURE 4.1 Map of Roman Greece and Asia Minor. Image created by author. Reproduced with permission of Accordance/Oak Tree Software, Inc.

from the same gods or heroes. When the writer to the Ephesians outlines the case for unity, he draws directly on this kind of civic tradition celebrating social harmony. He exhorts believers to be eager "to maintain the unity of the Spirit in the bond of peace. There is one body and one Spirit, just as you were called to the one hope of your calling, one Lord, one faith, one baptism, one God and Father of all, who is above all and through all and in all" (Eph. 4:3–6). The roughly contemporary orator and political philosopher Dio of Prusa (40–120 CE) attempted to resolve a dispute between the neighboring cities Nicomedia and Nicaea (near the Bosporus Strait) by reminding them of the bonds of "friendship and reconciliation and kinship" and urging them "to share in things which are good: unity of heart and mind."[1] Although couched in the differing discourses of Christian belief and politics, we see a remarkable overlap of ideals.

CITY GOVERNMENT

Rome conceived of its empire as a network of cities. Since the central power made do with only a very small class of high officials drawn from the senatorial class to govern the provinces, it had perforce to rely on local urban magistrates to assure collection of taxes and maintain public order. The effective deal was that Rome would ensure the frame conditions (peace and social order) that permitted the local city elites (perhaps 1.5% of the population) to extract income in the form of rents from the agrarian hinterland and use it at least in part for representative purposes within the city, thus providing employment for the craftsmen and other service providers resident in the city. Since, so far as we know, during the first century CE, Christians were found only in a few cities of the eastern Mediterranean, and in Rome itself, the following account is limited to a sketch of the situation in that part of the Greek-speaking Roman Empire, which had a long history of city organization within larger political entities, namely the Hellenistic kingdoms of Macedonia, the Attalid kingdom in west-central Asia Minor, and other minor independent kingdoms in the same region.

Politically, cities were ruled by annually elected magistrates who exercised their powers in accordance with the traditions of their respective city constitutions, but who were also expected to demonstrate loyalty to Rome and to collect imperial taxes from their administrative territories. This arrangement preserved their social status and protected their economic interests. It also guaranteed the means by which Rome retained political control over the urban populations governed on its behalf. This guarantee was accomplished by keeping direct taxation moderate in order to ensure that the urban wealthy could maintain social peace by providing their cities voluntarily with benefactions—more in large cities, and fewer in the many small cities—in the form of athletic competitions; gladiatorial games and beast hunts; chariot races; more or less elaborate religious festivals including free food and wine and music, dance, and theater performances; public buildings such as temples, baths, amphitheaters, theaters, libraries, and gymnasia; and distributions of food that reproduced the status hierarchy of the city. In times of food shortage it was expected that they would attempt to ameliorate the situation by purchasing grain abroad. Compulsory levies on magistrates, called "liturgies," included payments for the privilege of holding public office. Local priesthoods were also held by leading citizens, another indication that active citizenship encompassed both civic and sacral worlds. Wealthy citizens were expected, indeed required, to occupy political and religious offices. Those who resisted occupying them were reminded of their obligations. It is a typical feature of honorific cultures that those with more social power make expenditures on behalf of the larger community. This practice results in some, if limited, redistribution of resources, in return for which recipients bestow social power on their benefactors through public recognition and honors. In the urban world of the Roman Empire, such recognition usually took the form of inscriptions honoring donors with descriptions of their benefactions and the civic virtues they manifested. This system could survive so long as the balance between (imperial) tax and (local) rents was such that local elites were capable of such civic generosity. In the middle of the third century, with the arrival of plague, famine, imperial political instability in Rome, and military defeats, the edifice began to crumble.

We are accustomed to identify cities by their geographical location. First-century cities, however, were defined by their legal status. The Roman administration established a hierarchy of rank and privileges among the cities of the provinces of the Roman Empire. At the top were "colonies of Roman citizens" (*coloniae civium Romanorum*), whose populations in the Greek-speaking world were mainly descendants of military veterans settled in the period of the late Republican civil wars, but might also be freedpersons (as at Corinth) or Italians granted Roman citizenship. In the first century CE, Corinth and Philippi in Greece, along with Alexandreia Troas, Pisidian Antioch, Iconium, and Lystra in Asia Minor, enjoyed this privileged status. Their statutes contained precise definitions of the legal status of their inhabitants: Roman colonists, their wives, other Roman citizens, and then the *paroikoi* or *incoli*, who were *peregrini* (i.e., provincials without Roman or Latin status—the Greek-speaking and indigenous [non-Greek speaking] natives), and alien residents. The Christians in Roman colonies to whom Paul addressed his letters were most probably unprivileged inhabitants of this kind.

Lower in rank, but still privileged in terms of the range of tax liabilities, were cities that governed their internal affairs through their own laws, and which consequently had the right to call themselves "free." These included Thessalonica in northern

Greece, Smyrna and Tarsus in Asia Minor, and Antioch on the Orontes in Syria. Ephesus was never granted the status of colony but remained technically a "free" city, though subject to intervention by the governor as he saw fit. Even though it was the main residence of the Roman governor of the province of Asia, the site of a major jurisdiction (*conventus*), and the administrative headquarters of the tax office of Asia, with a sizeable Latin-speaking population.

The great majority of Greek cities, however, remained "peregrine" settlements subject to close supervision by the Roman governor and tax procurators. In legal terms, the populations of all these non-Roman cities were divided into several categories. At the top were free citizens, exclusively male, who had the right to belong to the civic assembly (usually termed *ekklēsia*). Indigenous women and children, although not members of the assembly, naturally enjoyed privileges as members of citizen families. Resident foreigners—*paroikoi*, or metics and itinerant aliens—and household slaves made up the remainder of the population. The preeminent right of citizens was to live in their home city. Their names were recorded on a register, they could own land and immovable property, and they had certain legal rights and privileges as well as civic obligations others did not have. It was possible to be a citizen in more than one city; moreover, additional citizenship in another city could be awarded for extraordinary acts and might even be purchased. Resident aliens were enrolled on a separate register, could participate in official civic events, and were required to shoulder part of the financial burden of municipal life. It is difficult to determine the typical proportions of citizens and noncitizens. In the case of Ephesus, whose population may have amounted to 100,000, one estimate suggests there may have been 22,000 free men, the same number of free women, 33,000 free children, and 22,000 slaves (the number of metics is impossible even to guess). Others argue that the number of local citizens in Ephesus was far smaller. The importance of the distinction between citizens and noncitizens is reflected in the way New Testament authors portray the status of believers. When the author of Ephesians celebrates the church as made of people who are "no longer strangers [*xenoi*] and resident aliens [*paroikoi*], but . . . fellow citizens [*sympolitai*] with the saints and also members of the household of God" (Eph. 2:19, NRSV, slightly revised), he is trading in political language to describe a new mode of incorporation into an alternative citizen body found in Christ.

In the Greek east official acts passed by the city (*polis*) were in the name of the "council and the people" (Greek: *boulē kai dēmos*). The council (there might be more than one), composed of present and past magistrates (i.e., members of the leading families), saw to all day-to-day business; the role of the "people," who met in the *ekklēsia*, was simply to affirm or acclaim the council's decisions. The New Testament uses the term *ekklēsia* to describe an assembly of Christians and is regularly translated as "church" in most Bibles. In modern usage, however, the word has lost all of its ancient political associations. To take the case of Ephesus, for example, a wealthy harbor city on the west coast of Asia Minor and, as we have seen, a "free" city, the body politic was a legally constituted and recognized *ekklēsia*. The passage at Ephesians 2:19 cited above celebrates the creation of a new body of citizens (*sympolitai*) in Christ. When Paul addresses letters to "the *ekklēsia* of God which is at Corinth" (1 Cor. 1:2; 2 Cor. 1:1), he uses a notably civic metaphor. One discovers further instances in the representation of Philippian believers as having their "citizenship [*politeuma*] in heaven" (Phil. 3:20) and in the reminder to the audience addressed by Hebrews that here it has no lasting city [*polis*], but looks to the one to come (Heb. 13:14). All of these passages speak to the urban dimensions of emergent Christian belief and express the idea not so much of a place as a new identity. Such language conferred upon women, slaves, and permanent and short-term residents a status otherwise denied them, and it may account in part for their attraction to the new religion.

Cities in the eastern Mediterranean, which had often developed independently from one another over several centuries, had their own unique officials and administrative structures, but in general each one had a constitution, city council (*boulē*), citizen assembly (*ekklēsia*), and annually elected magistrates (*archai*). City councils in some instances had as many as six hundred members, but they typically numbered around one hundred. Membership was restricted to those who possessed a certain amount of wealth, which resulted in a tendency toward oligarchy. The city council was composed of a greater variety of officers, such as secretaries (*grammateis*), treasurers (*tamiai*), festival directors (*agonothetai*), officials for keeping order (*eirenarchs*), gymnasium directors (*gymnasiarchs*), and so on. Members of the *ekklēsiastikoi*, as well as members of leading collegia or trade guilds (see below), were above the rest of the common citizens. We learn about a *grammateus* in Acts 19:35 who tries to bring order to a gathered assembly of citizens outraged that Paul's Gospel threatens dedication to the cult of Artemis. Here we should mention Erastus, the city treasurer (*oikonomos*) greeted by Paul in Romans 16:23. Some scholars have identified him as a civic official with the same name honored on a Corinthian inscription. If so, this would mean that at least one Christian in Corinth belonged to the lower-level civic elite, and was consequently a person of some wealth. But the name was a common one, and without any further evidence to corroborate the identification, there is no reason to suppose he was anything more than one of a number of public slaves and freedpersons who acted as magistrates' assistants.

Cities were sometimes part of federations or leagues (*koina*) that generally directed the imperial cult. *Asiarchs* were provincial officials of the cult; its priesthoods were prestigious positions occupied by wealthy men and women, sometimes for life and passed on to the next generation. Cities competed for the honor of hosting the cult and proudly advertised the privilege of doing so.

The Greek and Roman Mediterranean world was constituted by cultures in which the visual display of distinctions was a major means of measuring and affirming one's status in the social hierarchy—or, alternatively, of having one's insignificance openly affirmed. In its cities, public events such as religious festivals, games, and distributions of money and food were occasions for publicly marking hierarchical distinctions. For example, in public festivals where liturgies took the form of gifts of food or money, the amount one received depended directly upon one's rank. Likewise, seating at arenas and theaters was designated according to status. Such public events were a means of naturalizing the social order. Socialization was so successful that even among the poorest groups of artisans, members marked distinctions and displayed them among their peers by such means as the seating arrangement at meals, quantities of food and drink, honorific inscriptions, and so on. The Epistle of James rails against such status markers and the oppression of the poor they represent: "My brothers and sisters, do you with your acts of favoritism really believe in our glorious Lord Jesus Christ? For if a person with gold rings and in fine clothes comes into your assembly [*synagōgēn*], and if a poor person in dirty clothes also comes in, and if you take notice of the one wearing the fine clothes and say, 'Have a seat here, please,' while to the one who is poor you say, 'Stand there,' or, 'Sit at my feet,' have you not made distinctions among yourselves, and become judges with evil thoughts?" (James 2:1–4).

Paul advances a similar kind of reversal of expectations in 1 Corinthians 12:14–26, where, drawing on a traditional political metaphor, he likens the rightly functioning assembly of believers to a human body, with each of its parts performing its specific function for the harmonious functioning of the whole.

In its classical, Hellenistic, and Roman forms, head, arms, legs, and so on were seen as a naturally organized hierarchy the political order was to replicate. However, Paul inverts the trope by according greater honor to the "weaker," "less honorable," and "inferior" members (vv. 22–24). In the status-conscious world of Roman Corinth, Paul's teaching marks a dramatic reversal of expectations and invites a reconceptualization of the entire social order.

Turning to the more physical aspects of urban settlements of the Greek East, some were walled and accessed through gates that marked an urban center's main thoroughfares. The Roman peace, however, meant that many cities, such as Pergamum, felt they had no need of walls. The presence of walls and gates established the boundary separating town from country. These were sacred borders that helped confer a religious meaning on the territory inside a city's boundaries and protected the city's patron deities. Revelation 21:10–26 portrays a vivid image of the walls and gates of the heavenly Jerusalem and the presence of the slain lamb that lives in the city and assures the well-being of its residents. Its walls define the boundary between the sacred and the profane; outside them "are the dogs and sorcerers and fornicators and murderers and idolaters, and everyone who loves and practices falsehood" (22:15). Both Romans and Greeks buried their dead outside the city in order to avoid pollution, and in Revelation we see the author treating those outside the city gates as polluted and hence barred from entry. On the other hand, extramural graves were also a means to mark status. Those who could afford them buried their family members in monumental tombs that typically lined the thoroughfares leading to city gates, where passersby could read inscriptions and see images heralding the deceased for their virtues and benefactions. In Hebrews 13:12–14 the author draws on meanings associated with the physical boundaries of cities and provocatively reconceptualizes them in ways that draw on meanings associated with extramural pollution and honor. He reminds listeners that Jesus was executed outside the city gate of Jerusalem, and then exhorts them to follow him there and suffer the same abuse he endured, after which he instructs them that here they have no lasting city, and that they are to seek the city to come. The author here redefines civic sacred space by reversing the inside/outside meaning of city boundaries and locating the patron deity of the Christian assembly outside the city walls.

Eastern Mediterranean cities were filled with the same kind of monuments found in their Roman counterparts: forums, basilicas, temples, arenas, theaters, market squares, a bouleutērion, colonnaded avenues, and so on. Contact with Rome resulted in the advent of aqueducts, and with them came a new urban monument: the bathhouse. Ephesus had no less than three of them, and one combined with a gymnasium. The bathhouse-gymnasium complex at Sardis was one of the largest and most monumental public structures of the city, and it was copied by other cities. Alongside baths, the extension of ruler cult produced another type of monument alongside existing temples of Republican date to Roma or the Genius of the Senate and the Roman people: the *sebasteion,* or temple dedicated to the worship of the emperor. It was usually erected in the most prominent part of a city and transformed the urban landscape. In Ephesus a temple to the worship of the emperor Titus was built by his brother Domitian across from a sanctuary dedicated to Roma and Augustus. They were strategically located on either side of a central avenue used in festival processions dedicated to Artemis, the patron deity of the city. At Pergamum the temple for the worship of Trajan was built at the highest point of the acropolis and was visible for kilometers around.

In Asia Minor the gymnasium held pride of place for social events and daily gatherings. It was the center for *agones,* athletic and musical competitions, which probably every city staged. These were funded by the benefactions of wealthy magistrates and citizens who used them, among other things, as a means of currying favor among citizens in order to win votes for magistracies. In the honorific culture of the Mediterranean world, winning prizes at such athletic and artistic events conferred upon the victor the precious prize of social status and honor. The New Testament reveals its urban setting when it likens the life of faith to running races, boxing, winning prizes, and being crowned with victory (1 Cor. 9:24–25, 26; Gal. 2:2; 5.7; Phil. 2:16; 3:14; 1 Tim. 1:18; 6:12; 2 Tim 2:5; 4.7–8; see also Rom. 11:11). A sporting event and its spectators form the setting for the vivid exhortation of Hebrews 12:1: "Therefore, since we are surrounded by so great a cloud of witnesses, let us also lay aside every weight and the sin that clings so closely, and let us run with perseverance the race that is set before us." All of these passages reflect the centrality of festivals and competitive athletics in the daily life of full citizens.

Urban centers competed with one another for prestige and honors, especially as neokorate (honorific titles for cities boasting temples of the imperial cult) and *mētropolis* (top city in a specific province or *conventus*). In 26 CE there took place a famous debate in the Senate over which of the eleven major cities of the *koinon* of Asia was worthy of receiving the proposed temple in honor of Emperor Tiberius, which was finally granted to Smyrna. Cities were listed in a strict hierarchy of prestige and importance, and where magistrates from differing cities gathered, they were positioned according to their urban rank. One important place such rivalries were expressed, especially in Asia Minor, was at intercity games. These took place annually, biennially, or every four years, usually in association with sacred festivals. When the Paul of 2 Timothy says "no one is crowned without competing according to the rules" (2:5), or that "there is reserved for me the crown of righteousness, which the Lord, the righteous judge, will give me on that day" (4.8), he is borrowing imagery from games at religious festivals, where the winner was awarded a sacred crown dedicated to the gods. There were several sacred games, but from the first century onward the most important were those held in association with the imperial cult.

SIZE AND DENSITY

The proportion of the population of the empire that lived in cities is in sharp contrast with that of current demographic realities. Today, upward of 53% of humans reside in urban centers. In North America nearly 82% of the population lives in cities, and in Europe approximately 75% does.[2] Additionally, the size of modern cities contrasts with that of ancient ones. In 2014 there were twenty-eight cities with populations over ten million, 500 exceeding one million, and almost 5,000 over 100,000.[3] People in the ancient world could not conceive of such vast numbers. The Roman Empire contained approximately 2,000 cities, most of them in the eastern Mediterranean, Italy, and North Africa. There were five megacities; the largest, Rome, had between 500,000 and one million inhabitants, followed by Alexandria (possibly up to 500,000), Antioch on the Orontes in Syria (150,000), and Carthage and Ephesus (somewhere between 100,000 and 250,000). Corinth's population may have been 90,000; that of Thessalonica 30,000, and Jerusalem 20,000. These last two are exceptions; unlike the modern world, there were few cities of intermediate size. The bulk of the empire's cities were by modern standards very small, more like villages or tiny towns of 5,000 to 10,000. Philippi may have had a population of 10,000, Laodicea 13,350, and Hierapolis 7,350.

One important feature of these numbers relates to urban density and human contact. Contemporary urban living is largely anonymous. Neighbors often do not know each other's names, and modern urban residents travel across cities or further still to visit friends and relatives, or they are a mouse click away from face-to-face conversation with people who live on the other side of the planet. The ancient urban world was very different. In smaller cities of five to ten thousand, where the majority of people were born and died in the same place, we can expect that social networks were local and close at hand, and that people were more or less recognizable to one another. The references in 1 Peter to the persecution of Christians are perhaps telling in this regard. The letter addresses itself to a group of Christians living in one or more small cities of thinly urbanized eastern Bithynia and Pontus (i.e., the southern coast of the Black Sea). The author exhorts, "[I]f any of you suffers as Christians, do not consider it a disgrace, but glorify God because you bear his name" (4:16). Here the epithet "Christian" is a slur probably coined by non-Christians to caricature a suspect new religion. A local face-to-face context of the insult can be assumed from 4:4, where the author states, "They [namely urban unbelievers] are surprised that you no longer join them in the same excesses of dissipation [described in v. 3], and so they blaspheme." In a smaller community, Christians would have been conspicuous, especially by their absence if they refused to participate in the public religious festivals that were a major feature of urban life.

Another important consideration when studying the differences between Roman and modern cities is population density. In 2018 the three most densely populated cities measured in residents/square kilometer were Dhaka, Bangladesh, (47,400), Mogadishu, Somalia, (28,600), and Al-Raqqa, Syria (27,200). London (5,600) and Chicago (1,300) represent significantly lower population densities.[4] Comparison with ancient urban densities is instructive. If Ephesus had a population of 100,000 spread over 2.25 square kilometers, it had an urban density of 44,444. Rome, with a population of 1 million occupying 14

More density in Roman cities

square kilometers within the Aurelian walls, had one of 71,429, a density 1.5 times that of Dhaka. To accommodate these numbers, Roman families of typically five to seven people were piled into five-story tenement buildings, and lived in rented rooms of typically 30–50 square meters that had no heating, running water, or cooking or toilet facilities. The archaeological evidence of urban housing in the other large cities of the Roman Empire suggests similar patterns. Anecdotal evidence also supports this picture. The Bible's only near fatality from a sermon assumes some kind of apartment building at the port city of Alexandreia Troas. Eutychus plummets to the ground from a third-floor window when he falls asleep listening to Paul's preaching (Acts 20:9–12). After assuring his listeners that the young man is not dead but only unconscious, the apostle returns upstairs to continue his sermon. Nevertheless, Rome was exceptional. A more representative lower-range city like Hierapolis in Phrygia, had a population of 7,350 spread over .5 square kilometers, an urban density greater than that of London. Even if one is more conservative in these estimates and halves urban density, or argues that residents lived outside city walls and boundaries, one still arrives at population densities that exceed modern American, European, and even Asian averages. Further, all of these figures assume an evenly distributed density, but at least 10% of the area of many cities was given over to civic or public buildings such as temples, markets, baths, gymnasia, arenas, theaters, and so on. The take-away is that while ancients may not have been able to imagine the sizes of our cities, it lies outside the bounds of the typical First World imagination to comprehend the urban crowding, to say nothing of the mortality rates, of ancient ones.

Once off the beaten track of a city's main thoroughfares, narrow streets carved up the city. From this fact we can assume that life was lived around one's neighborhood. One model of the imperial urban city suggests that the poor, clients, former slaves, and those economically dependent on fulfilling the appetites of the wealthy lived cheek by jowl with the residences of the rich, where they could take advantage of economic opportunities. Unlike modern cities where the wealthy and poor live in separate neighborhoods, the rich and poor of the Roman Empire lived alongside or, in the case of *insulae*, on top of each other. As we can see from ancient Ostia, the port of Rome, a typical urban apartment block, or *insula* (Figure 4.2), comprised shops, or *tabernae* on the ground floor, where their owners and families often lived, larger apartments on the second floor for richer people, who paid their rent annually or semiannually, and multi- or single-room dwellings on the upper floors that were usually rented out by the day or week. This housing made for densely packed living quarters and, through the visible display of status, a reinforcement of social distinctions.

This meant that life was constantly on public view. Paul reflects this when he advises the Corinthians not to exercise the gift of glossolalia all at once and exhorts them to be more orderly. Part of his concern is what neighbors will think if they

FIGURE 4.2 Scale model of a 4 and 2 storey Roman *insula*, Ostia, first century CE. The facing foundations are of other *insulae* and reveal the narrow streets dividing the buildings. Photo by author. Museo della civiltà Roma, Rome.

hear everyone engaging in ecstatic speech together. "If . . . outsiders or unbelievers enter, will they not say that you are out
of your mind?" (1 Cor. 14:23). In a situation of cheek-by-jowl
living, such a possibility would have been great. Cramped
urban conditions probably also occasioned suspicion when
Christians conducted rituals open only to initiates (the baptized). A typical charge by detractors of the second and
third centuries can be seen in a Christian apology written by
Minucius Felix (second to third century) that records an imagined conversation in Ostia between a Roman non-Christian,
Caecilius, and a Christian, Octavius. Caecilius rehearses common
rumors that Christians have initiatory rights where they can-
nibalize infants "at their clandestine and nocturnal ceremonies." He goes on to accuse them of engaging in orgies as he
describes the regular Christian practice of participating in
multigenerational and mixed-gender agape meals or love banquets that included the Eucharist.[5] This kind of rumor-based
accusation probably arose in part due to closed-door religious
practices in crowded neighborhoods and tenement buildings.

One of the consequences of imperial urban density was
that life was lived largely out of doors, at public places such as
market places, baths, arenas, and gymnasia. It is not surprising
that several episodes of Paul's life depicted in the Book of Acts
reflect the outdoor urban life of imperial city residents. Luke
often portrays the apostle teaching in synagogues and households, but public settings also serve as the backdrop for his
teaching and ministry. At Lystra he heals a disabled man living
on the street (Acts 14:8–13). In Philippi, Paul and Silas seek recruits by the riverside near the city gate (Acts 16:13). Later we
see Paul in Athens talking "in the market place every day with
those who chanced to be there" (17:17), and then on the hill of
the Areopagus, where he engages a crowd who "spent their time
in nothing except telling or hearing something new" (17:16–21).
The narrator presents Paul at Ephesus arguing daily at the hall

of Tyrannus, possibly a reference to a part of the gymnasium where Ephesians gathered to exercise and converse (19:9).

Overcrowded urban living is not the first thing that usually comes to mind when one imagines the cities of the Roman Empire or reads a New Testament letter addressed to an assembly of first-century Christians. Modern tourists who travel to biblical sites such as Rome, Ephesus, or Corinth gain no real sense of the social world of typical urban residents. They see what the imperial urban wealthy left for them to view: the monuments they erected in order to win the precious social commodity of honor. This is the airbrushed imperial city that hides the ugly reality of what city life was like for the vast majority of its residents. Were we to be transported in time to a typical city street, the first thing we would notice would not be the monuments, but the stench of sewage, since, even with Roman plumbing, most urban dwellers deposited their waste on the street. Next, perhaps, we would notice the poverty of most of the urban population living at or just above subsistence. We would see a largely young population, since few people lived past forty, and among those we would notice a low level of personal hygiene and a high degree of malnutrition and sickness, as well as homelessness. We would see crowded shops and apartment buildings situated along narrow streets as well as ramshackle housing propped up where there was available space. We would find it hard to get from one place to another because of the crush of people. We might see people living under bridges, in doorways, under stairs, in taverns and shops, in the tombs that surrounded cities—anywhere they might find shelter. Finally, we would see a good deal of death. Without benefit of knowledge of germs, antibiotics, or protection against disease when sickness came to a city, it spread quickly through the cramped urban quarters of overcrowded ancient cities. Children were most vulnerable. Half of all children died before the age of ten (some argue before the age of two). Such typical urban scenes furnish a striking social backdrop to the verse from Hebrews in which the author tells listeners that here they have no lasting city. They hardly needed to be reminded: if they were typical urban residents, their earthly city was a constant lesson in the precarious and fragile nature of daily life. This is a far cry from marble settings and pristine toga-wearing aristocrats we are primed by modern entertainment to imagine as the backdrop for the typical people living in the Roman cities of the New Testament world. It is only when we enter the crowded, brutal realities of ancient city life that we can begin to understand the urban conditions of early Christianity, as well as how an ethic centered in hospitality and care of the destitute might have attracted new believers.

URBAN ECONOMIES

Most of the churches named in the New Testament were at or close to the west and south coasts of Asia Minor and the east coast of Greece, where classical and Hellenistic urbanization had been most intense. Their location is explained by the presence of accessible farmland and the existence of major river valleys. Laodicea, Hierapolis, and Colossae, for example, were located in the fertile Lycus River valley. Although many Greek cities grew in size and prosperity under the Principate (we know of about five hundred that at some point issued their own coinage for local use), almost none were first foundations. Among other things, increased urbanization indicates the economic effect Rome was having on the Mediterranean world. That picture is confirmed in literary sources. Writing in the second century, the rhetorician Aelius Aristides, in a speech praising the city of Rome, says,

> Here is brought from every land and sea all the crops of the season and the produce of each land, river, lake, as well as of the arts

of the Greeks and barbarians, so that if someone should wish to
view all these things, he must either see them by traveling over
the whole world or be in this city. . . . So many merchant ships ar-
rive here, conveying every kind of goods from every people every
hour and every day, so that the city is like a factory common to
the whole earth.[6]

A close look at the size and distribution of town and urban
settlements in Asia Minor shows an economy functioning to
make possible the kind of picture Aristides presents. One sees
smaller settlements, (villages, festival centers, rural markets)
serving as focal points for the collection of primary produce
due as rent and tax, which was then moved, apparently by the
tax farmers, to larger centers where they were consumed or
stored (i.e., retained by members of the local elite in the hope of
higher prices), or in some cases, if there were a harbor nearby,
shipped further afield.

Furthermore, in mainland Greece at any rate, we find an increased level of nucleation, or abandonment of ancestral farms
for residence closer to the city. Of the many factors that motivated people to move, three are noteworthy for our discussion
here. The first is that there was a minimum size beneath which
a peasant holding was no longer capable of supporting a family.
Once a farm had reached that size, excess children would have
to be got rid of, either by exposure, sale to other families who
would bring up such a child as a house slave, forced (very early)
marriages of daughters, or simply requiring surplus sons to
leave the farm once the value of their labor was outweighed
by the cost of keeping them. Once they left, they would have
few other alternatives other than to move to a nearby city, join
a band of robbers, or be recruited into the auxiliary troops of
army. Secondly, wealthy landholders tended, by dint of several
different strategies—advantageous marriages with heiresses, exploitation of their role as tax collectors for the Roman authorities,

management of famine periods and peasant indebtedness—to increase the size of their landholdings, reducing free peasants to tenants and sharecroppers. Of course, it was not at all in the interests of large landholders to lose agricultural labor, but some members of peasant families would eventually drift into cities to join the underemployed artisan workforce there. Although much Roman tax collection (like rents) was in kind, the poll tax was usually required to be paid in money, so that the incorporation of an area into the Roman economy meant a need for more cash. According to one well-known model of the Roman economy, this tended to force peasants, the primary producers, despite their situation as subsistence farmers, to place more agricultural produce on the market and so increase their dependence on central places, including cities. Although nowhere mentioned in the New Testament, it is not unreasonable to imagine these more migrant populations spreading Christianity into the countryside after their conversion in a city, perhaps as a result of supplementing income by taking on work to assist with harvests on larger estates.

Most of the urban settlements of the Roman Empire were cities of consumption; that is, the agricultural production of the primary producers supported the population of the city, both a handful of the rich, who owned much of the land, and the artisans, service providers, and other workers who produced goods and services either for these wealthier residents or to support agricultural production (mainly the provision of iron tools and plowshares). We can distinguish others types of settlement, of which the most important are those that specialized in particular types of valued product; these include, most notably, Ephesus, Pergamum, Corinth, and Thessalonica. In either case, urban centers played a critical role in fashioning imperial identity. Aristides gives us an idealized and exaggerated account of this set of social arrangements. The Book of Revelation takes a different view, as we saw in the last chapter, where we saw John describe the luxury goods passing through Asia Minor (Rev. 18:11–19). Here the list of wares, including slaves, speaks to both urban consumption by the wealthy and economic brutality.

THE DISTRIBUTION OF WEALTH

A far larger majority might have had more sympathy for John's critique than Aristide's glowing assessment. A recent model of the economic demography of the Roman Empire, developed by Steven Friesen, is instructive in this regard (see Table 4.1). Friesen divides up the Roman imperial population into seven socioeconomic levels and assigns a percentage to each.[7] The question marks indicate where there is a level of uncertainty in the estimate.

The picture that emerges from this model is that the imperial population was constituted by a fraction of the super wealthy

Table 4.1

FRIESEN'S POVERTY INDEX

Poverty Scale	Economic Level	Population (%)
PS1	Imperial elites	0.04
PS2	Regional or provincial elite	1.00
PS3	Municipal elites	1.76
PS4	Moderate surplus	7.00?
PS5	Stable near subsistence	22.00?
PS6	At subsistence	40.00
PS7	Below subsistence	28.00

Source: Adapted from Steven J. Friesen, "Poverty in Pauline Studies: Beyond the So-Called New Consensus," *Journal for the Study of the New Testament* 26, no. 3 (2004): 323–61, at 341. Reprinted with permission from the author.

surrounded by a mass of the poor. A slightly later model, developed by Friesen and Walter Scheidel, offers a more nuanced account of the distribution of imperial wealth by giving attention to what they call a "middling group," a population that corresponds to PS4 in Table 4.1 (see Table 4.2). This model takes into consideration wealth, prices, elite wealth, and per capita GDP. This is especially important for the discussion of the city and its residents undertaken here because of the breakdown of the middling group and the fact, as we will see, that we should place at least some urban Christians within this category.

On this model, the wealthiest households, comprising 1.5% of the population, controlled 20% of the empire's wealth; the middling group (Friesen's PS4), approximately 10% of the

Table 4.2

A MODEL OF THE ROMAN ECONOMY BASED ON A POPULATION OF 54–60 MILLION PRODUCING 50 MILLION TONS OF WHEAT/YEAR OR 20 BILLION SESTERCES/YEAR (GDP)

Economic Group	Population (%)	Control of Total Income (%)
State and local government	<1	5
Elite households	1.5	20
Middling groups	10*	20
People just above, at, or below subsistence⁺	88**	55

⁺Subsistence = 2100 calories/day.
*2%: 5–10 levels above subsistence; 8%: 1–3.5 levels above subsistence.
**8%: .25–.66 levels above subsistence; 60%: at or close to subsistence; 20%: below subsistence; <.25%: starvation level.
Source: Adapted from Walter Scheidel and Steven J. Friesen, "The Size of the Economy and the Distribution of Income in the Roman Empire," *Journal of Roman Studies* 99 (2009): 61–91. Reprinted with permission from the authors.

population, controlled 20% of total wealth; while the vast majority (88%) lived just above, at, or below subsistence.

This account shows a significant amount of economic power (25%) controlled by wealthy households and middling groups who are either better-off farmers or urban dwellers living at least one level higher than subsistence. The model breaks down the "middling" section into five levels to reveal an income distribution that depended, among other things, on whether one was a skilled or unskilled worker. Of this 10%, 2% lived anywhere from five to ten times above the level of subsistence, and the rest lived three to just over one level over it. From these calculations we can imagine an urban population composed of a tiny body of elites; a small but economically significant middling group, of whom the majority lived near subsistence; and a vast number of both urban and rural populations (88%) living at or below subsistence, who nevertheless generated 65% of the empire's wealth. Scheidel and Friesen's figures are consistent with independently constructed economic models of other preindustrial cities. In the case of the Roman Empire, they represent an economic set of factors that any discussion of the city and its residents must take into account in order to get a feel for life on the ground in imperial urban centers.

ARTISANS

Friesen and Scheidel assume that the more prosperous members of the middling groups were either prosperous farmers or urban artisans who could take advantage of the economic opportunities created by the improved communicative space of the empire. This is an important observation because, as we will see, there is abundant evidence that many Christians were artisans and merchants, and that a strong case can be made that some of them may have been people who belonged to the upper 2%

of the middling group. One scholar has identified the artisans and shopkeepers of the Roman Empire as forming a "taberna economy," named after the shops lining market places and streets throughout the cities, towns, and villages of the empire.[8] Evidence of increases in both production and consumption of wares across the Empire is indicative of how well some of these shopkeepers were doing in the imperial economy.

There is a debate among scholars concerning which kind of living arrangement was the more typical form for urban Christians. Starting in the 1980s a consensus emerged that the typical house churches of Christians were urban villas where wealthy patrons welcomed believers for worship and common meals. Scholars have recently challenged this view as too one-sided and economically inflated, given the high number of Greco-Roman urban residents living at subsistence. In the alternative portrait, the typical life setting of urban Christian assemblies was probably not a villa, however modest, but a workshop or some other small rented room. It seems better to err on the side of caution. While it is indeed the case that in this period urban artisans and merchants profited from new opportunities, the New Testament seems to point in several directions and suggests that Christians lived under a variety of economic conditions. This is what one would predict using Friesen and Scheidel's economic model.

At an upper level of the middling group, we might place a Christian like Philemon. He owned a slave, Onesimus, and was host to Paul and the church (Philem. 2). Alongside him we might include Stephanas, who had the resources to travel and make his household resources available for service in the Gospel, possibly a reference to loaning the services of a slave (1 Cor. 16:15–18). We might also include here Crispus, who according to Acts 18:8 was an *archisynagogos*, or synagogue official, often an office held by a person of some means. Finally we can point to Jason, a host of Paul and Silas at Thessalonica, with sufficient funds to post bail after they were arrested in Thessalonica (Acts 17:6–9).

Perhaps he is the kind of person alluded to in Acts 17:12, where Luke numbers among Paul's converts in Macedonia "not a few women and men of high standing." Luke's representation of Paul in Acts as a literate, educated "tentmaker" (18.3; probably a weaver of cloth or a leather worker) and, perhaps more importantly, as a Roman citizen may suggest that the apostle commanded a higher level of economic power. When we look at noncanonical Christian literature contemporary with the New Testament, a similar picture emerges. In *The Shepherd of Hermas*, a writing from late first- to mid-second-century Rome, a freedman and Roman Christian named Hermas receives numerous visions warning that the members of his assembly are too concerned with their business dealings and not enough with their poorer brothers and sisters. "Avoid excessive involvement in business, and you will commit no sin," warns Hermas's heavenly messenger, the Shepherd. "For those who are involved in business a great deal also sin a great deal, since they are distracted by their business and do not serve their own Lord in anything."[9] In an earlier vision in the same work, the Shepherd admonishes some wealthier Roman Christians, "If, therefore, you know your city in which you are destined to live, why do you prepare fields and expensive possessions and buildings and useless rooms here? If you are preparing these things for this city, you obviously are not planning to return to your own city."[10]

Alongside these references we should include the interesting evidence of women of some means in the service of Paul's Gospel. In Romans 16:1–2, Paul recommends that Christians in Rome welcome one of his associates, Phoebe, whom he goes on to describe as a benefactor (*prostatis*) of him and many others. It is possible that she is bringing Paul's letter to Rome while attending to other business in the capital. A merchant of greater wealth was Lydia, a woman from Thyatira, whom Acts 16:14–15 describes as a "dealer in purple cloth [*porphyropōlis*]," converted together with her household by Paul. Another female merchant of some importance was Prisca (Priscilla), named by both Paul (Rom. 16:3; 1 Cor. 16:19; see also 2 Tim. 4:19) and Acts (18:2–3, 18, 26). These merchants, together with Paul, ply their trade as "tentmakers" at Corinth (Acts 18:3; Rom 16:3) and act as benefactors by hosting the church "in their house" (i.e., probably a rented taberna or workshop). Another benefactor was Nympha, whom Colossians 4:15 singles out as host to the church. Phoebe, Lydia, and possibly Prisca are examples of women active in trades and commerce. Arguably, the women Paul names would have found in Paul's Gospel proclamation of there no longer being male and female in Christ a transcendence of the kind of gender codes by which they were living in their larger social world. Outside of Paul's letters, there are also references to women of means in Acts. Luke numbers "wives of first [citizens]" and "respected or noble [euschēmonai]" women among the first converts to Christianity in Thessalonica and nearby Beroea (Acts 17:4, 12). However, Luke has a tendency to inflate the social status of the first believers in Christ, so these may be exaggerated descriptions.

These are examples of people who possibly possessed some degree of wealth at least at the level of the middling 2%, if not higher. There is also evidence, however, of poor urban artisans who were in the lower 8%. The majority of a city's artisans were unskilled workers, service providers, and craftspeople engaging in small-scale production to meet the needs of the city and its surrounding farms, who also often hired themselves out as laborers during harvest season. Outside the New Testament period, Origen cites extensively the anti-Christian polemic of a second-century Greek philosopher, Celsus, who pilloried Christians as "wool-workers, cobblers, laundry-workers, and the most illiterate and bucolic yokels, who would not dare to say anything at all in front of their elders and more intelligent masters." He goes on to describe how they seek to win over recruits at "the wool dresser's shop, or [at] the cobbler's or the washerwoman's shop," where potential new believers hope to find perfection.[11] The trades listed are those of mostly unskilled and uneducated local producers for urban and surrounding country residents. Artisans were the frequent butt of humor of the more literate class, and so Celsus's description may be rhetorical. However, it is confirmed to some degree by Paul's reference to his work in Thessalonica. He is probably describing laboring alongside a local workshop of artisans as he recalls proclaiming his Gospel there (1 Thess. 2:9; also 1 Cor. 4:12, for Corinth), and it is to laborers that he directs his exhortation "to mind your own affairs, and to work with your hands" (1 Thess. 4:11; also 2 Thess. 3:12). These are the urban poor; in 2 Corinthians 8:2 he is describing Christians in Thessalonica when he alludes to the "extreme poverty" of Macedonian believers. Paul lists among his trials the suffering typical of the artisans of his day living at or slightly above subsistence, exhausting toil, and the need to work during both day and night (1 Thess. 2:9; also 2 Thess. 3:8). Similarly expressive of subsistence living is his catalogue of hardships in the Corinthian correspondence: toil, cold (2 Cor. 11:27), poor clothing, labors, hunger and thirst (1 Cor. 4:11; 2 Cor. 6:5; 11:27), and nakedness (1 Cor. 4:11; 2 Cor. 11:27). Such references are a far cry from a villa owner, the slave-owning Philemon, or the enterprising woman Phoebe.

URBAN ASSOCIATIONS

Many residents of Greek cities belonged to groups that occupied an intermediate position between the civic world and the family, namely voluntary associations. These went by a variety of terms, including *koinon* (association), *thiasos* (society), *synodos* (group), *eranos* (club), *orgeōnes* (sacrificing associates), *synagōgos, ekklēsia*, and *oikos* (the final three words also used to describe Christian and Jewish gatherings). They were formed for a variety of purposes. Some gathered extended family members, others met around a common cult or a shared diasporic identity. They could consist of people sharing the same occupation, perhaps in the form of neighborhood associations made up of trades located in a particular part of a town. The number of members might range from a dozen or less to several hundred. In some, membership transcended social divisions to include free men, women, freedpersons, and even slaves, thus furnishing a compelling analogy with Christian assemblies similarly marked by socioeconomic diversity. An association might also play a part in the civic assembly. We see this distinction in action in Acts 19:23–41, where Demetrius, a silversmith who makes idols for the cult of Artemis, joins with "workers of the same trade" (v. 25) to gather the assembly at the theater in order to condemn Paul's companions Gaius and Aristarchus. Demetrius is worried that the apostle threatens his and his colleagues' business (v. 27).

Some of these informal associations met regularly for banquets and other meetings, and most engaged in cultic activities. Many paid for the burial of members. They were governed by an elected hierarchy of officials, who often held the same civic and religious titles as the magistrates of cities. Associations typically had a constitution that defined the means of admission, the payment of dues, a code of conduct (whose language often parallels the prescriptions and prohibitions found in New Testament virtue and vice lists), and disciplinary actions that included fines and even expulsion for bad behavior. They often had patrons who were named in inscriptions honoring them for their benefactions. It was possible to belong to more than one association, although some, especially religious associations, tried to limit membership to their group alone. It is more than possible that when Paul challenges Corinthian Christians for eating idol food in temple dining rooms (1 Cor. 8:10; 10:20–21), he is referring to participation in an association that engages in cultic activity. Ancient depictions of people banqueting beneath scenes of sacrifice or in the company of patron deities (see Figure 4.3) furnish a remarkable visual representation of what Paul and his listeners would have imagined when the apostle referred to sitting at the table of Christ and sharing his body and blood, or being a partner at the table of demons (1 Cor. 10:16, 21). The monument of a village association from Asia Minor shows reclining banqueters entertained by dancers and musicians with depictions of Zeus, Artemis, and Apollo above. Many scholars discover in Greco-Roman associations the closest analogies for the worshiping and dining activities of urban Christian assemblies, as well as the gatherings of Diaspora Jews for worship in synagogues. Alongside the depictions of banqueting, there are interesting parallels between the titles of leaders of Christian churches (overseer [*episkopos*], elder [*presbyteros*], attendant [*diakonos*], manager [*proistamenos*], leader [*hēgoumenos*], and so on) and those of association officials.

Associations met in a variety of places. Often they rented a hall or a temple dining room. Other meetings took place in tabernae or artisan workshops. Some religious associations met in homes where family members also functioned as religious officials of the domestic cult. Wealthier guilds sometimes undertook the construction of a temple in honor of a patron deity and met in an adjacent hall or dining room. In some areas they gradually took over an *insula* or apartment block that became identified with their trade or occupation. There is intriguing evidence that the formula "at the house of" (*kat' oikon*), a phrase Paul used to describe a Christian assembly (Rom. 16:5; 1 Cor. 16:19; Col. 4:15; Philem. 2), was also used to describe an association meeting place. In such instances the reference is to a workshop at an *insula*, though the word *oikos* can also mean a single room in a larger building. This range of meanings calls into question traditional New Testament scholarship that considers these references to stand-alone house churches or villas. One important piece of evidence used to argue for

FIGURE 4.3 Village association relief, Mysia, first century BCE–second century CE. From M. Perdrizet, "Reliefs mysiens," *Bulletin de correspondance hellénique* 23 (1899), 592–3, plate IV, in public domain.

Christian hosts welcoming believers into their villas is the reference to Gaius in Rom. 16:23. The argument rests on a problematic translation that describes Gaius as "host to me [Paul] and the whole church" (NRSV; other translations render the Greek roughly equivalently). This is customarily interpreted to mean that there are several house churches that have separate meetings but periodically convene together for one large one in Gaius's Corinthian villa or luxury apartment. However, as has recently been argued, Paul in Rom. 16:23 does not use the Greek word host (*xenodochos*) to describe Gaius, but the word for guest (*xenos*). This has led to the suggestion that the apostle and the entire Corinthian church has welcomed Gaius, arguably a visitor from Rome—an otherwise attested practice of associations in the Roman Empire.[12] There is no reason, therefore, to think of Gaius having a villa or a house large enough to gather all the Corinthian Christians. Rather we might imagine him as a guest of Paul and a group of believers who live in, at, or near a Corinthian *insula* or other multi-residence complex. Such assemblies would have been small, perhaps with no more than one to three dozen members.

JEWS AND GOD-FEARERS

We turn now to the question of the civic identity of Jews in Greco-Roman cities, their legal privileges, and the degree of integration into municipal life. First, there is ample evidence that Jews could be both citizens and elected urban officials, and that they furnished cities with benefactions. Second, in a few cities, most famously Alexandria, the Jewish population had the status of a *politeuma*; that is, it enjoyed a degree of political and legal autonomy and was governed by its own magistrates, senate, and elders. In this case the term designates a formal set of legal rights and recognition as a religious assembly. It also parallels a widespread and local designation of status found in inscriptions from Greek cities where resident aliens from the same city or region formed an association and defined themselves as a *politeuma*. Such *politeumata* could consist of people from the same ethnic group or region plying a common trade or worshiping their native deity. These groups were formed on an ad hoc basis.

Their existence calls into question an oft-repeated assertion that Jews in the Roman Empire enjoyed a kind of blanket legal identity as a permitted religion, or *religio licita*. The evidence points instead to a reality closer to the local recognition of other diasporic associations. This reality indicates that there was no overarching imperial law preserving Jewish rights of religion or assembly. Rather, like other local groups of citizens, permanent residents, and itinerant aliens, associations of Jews advanced their interests in more local ways. This idea challenges the theory that early Christianity fell prey to Roman persecution once it parted ways with Judaism, and thereby no longer enjoyed the cloak of a legally approved religion. Leaving aside the anachronism of naming the diversity of belief and practice of Jews in the empire as a single "Judaism," this notion confuses purely local arrangements with formal decisions by imperial rescript or senatorial rulings (*consulta*), and it ignores the analogies with other similar ethnic groups living as permanent or casual residents in cities.

This is not to deny that the privileges that urban Jews sought or exercised were distinct from other diasporic citizens. Of special concern was the right to collect the tax Jews were required by their ancestral laws to pay to the temple in Jerusalem. A second was Sabbath observance, since it meant freedom from civic responsibilities and obligations (such as appearing in court) on the Jewish day of rest. Exemption from holding priesthoods, a typical obligation among leading citizens, as well as other liturgies, was paid for by a legally agreed upon fee. In order to achieve these dispensations and to promote their community's interests, Jewish citizens needed to be adept at negotiating the politics of urban assemblies and councils. Nonparticipation in civic religious festivals remained an issue. Jews attacked by hostile groups sought legal protection by appealing to the legal exemptions they had won from local magistrates. The evidence again points to ad hoc urban and not empire-wide policies.

Like other groups, Jews used public gestures to gain recognition and benefits. For example, a number of communities of Jews in the Roman province of Asia, engaging in the common practice among associations of passing a decree (*psēphisma*) in praise of a benefactor, wrote a formal letter to Emperor Augustus praising him for his excellent administration and virtues, possibly in a situation of increasing pressure upon Jewish groups in the province. In response, the emperor issued an edict confirming Julius Caesar's affirmation of Jewish rights and explicitly forbidding interference with the dispatch of the Temple tax to Jerusalem and the theft of Jewish holy texts. He ordered that the original letter and the edict be displayed (i.e., inscribed) in the temple of Roma and Augustus (the *sebasteion*) at Ancyra in Galatia.[13]

This interaction represents a typical case of the trading of honors and benefactions that formed the basic currency of imperial public life. Urban Jews also posted honorific inscriptions. One from Akmoneia in Asia Minor honors Julia Severa, an aristocrat who was also a priestess in the imperial cult, for building a local synagogue. This parallels the report in Luke of a centurion building a synagogue in Capernaum (Luke 7:1–5). These echo other instances of groups in imperial cities enjoying the patronage of outsiders not sharing their regional, ethnic, or religious association identity.

Although Jews belonged to a diasporic community or synagogue, they were sometimes also members of other associations. One funerary inscription from Hierapolis in Phrygia, dated 190–220 CE, records Glykon, a deceased Jew and Roman citizen, leaving money for an impressive variety of purposes—to have an association of purple dyers ceremonially crown his grave and share in a banquet at the Jewish festival of Unleavened Bread, to dispense additional funds for the grave crowning to a synod of carpet weavers, and to distribute funds during the Roman festival of the Kalends (presumably of January) and at the Jewish celebration of Pentecost. This fine example of multiple association memberships being held by a member of a Jewish synagogue association is remarkable in that he funds both a Roman and a Jewish celebration.

Multiple affiliations also went the other way. The Book of Acts portrays god-fearers as the first gentile Christians (Acts 10:2; 13:16; 16:14; 17:4, 17; 18:7). The term "god-fearer" was used widely in the ancient world to describe a person dedicated to a deity. When used by Jews it referred to sympathizers to Judaism, who attended or were patrons of synagogues, but who were not proselytes (i.e., uncircumcised and not keeping Jewish dietary regulations or strict observance of Sabbath and other legal regulations). Many god-fearers connected with Judaism participated in religious cults in addition to joining in the worship at synagogues. Such multiple associations are perhaps implied where Paul reminds gentile Christians of their former idolatry, often in arguments that presume a good familiarity with the Hebrew Bible on their part (e.g., Gal. 4:21–31; 1 Cor. 10:1–10).

As Christianity became embedded in the households, workshops, and ultimately the neighborhoods of the imperial urban world, Christians faced the same challenges that Jews had faced when they, in Diaspora communities, tried to live out their civic and religious commitments in contexts that were, from a religious perspective, inimical to their beliefs.

What were the appropriate—and prudent—ways to take part in the urban life of the cities to which believers were undoubtedly loyal while, at the same time, distancing themselves from the round of religious activities typically associated with urban practice (whether in the larger setting of urban festivals or in local associations)? That question would challenge Christians for centuries.

THE HOUSEHOLD AND ITS

MEMBERS

[T]he appointed time has grown short; from now on, let even those who have wives be as though they had none.

—*1 Corinthians 7:29*

Wives, be subject to your husbands, as is fitting in the Lord. Husbands, love your wives and never treat them harshly. Children, obey your parents in everything, for this is your acceptable duty in the Lord. Fathers, do not provoke your children, or they may lose heart. Slaves, obey your earthly masters in everything, not only while being watched and in order to please them, but wholeheartedly, fearing the Lord. Whatever your task, put yourselves into it, as done for the Lord and not for your masters, since you know that from the Lord you will receive the inheritance as your reward; you serve the Lord Christ. For the wrongdoer will be paid back for whatever wrong has been done, and there is no partiality. Masters, treat your slaves justly and fairly, for you know that you also have a Master in heaven.

—*Colossians 3:18–4.1*

THIS CHAPTER TURNS TO A discussion of the household of the Greco-Roman world and its members. To enter into the domestic world of antiquity is quickly to discover oneself in a foreign world. First, there is the issue of nomenclature and hierarchy. The Greek and Latin words for household and family (*oikos, oikia* and *domus, familia,* respectively) refer to entities far different from contemporary Western understandings, where such terms traditionally refer to a nuclear family and its property. In the ancient world they designated a wider set of realities that included slaves, former slaves or freedpersons, matrilineal and patrilineal ties and laws, and a series of obligations of one set of members to others. We can see this expanded understanding of household and family in a series of New Testament and extrabiblical, as well as Greek and Jewish, texts that biblical scholars call "household codes." The passage from Colossians cited above is representative of these codes. Together with other similar New Testament passages (Eph. 5:22–6:9 1 Pet. 2:18–3:7; also 1 Tim. 2:8–15; 3:2–13; Titus 1:5–9), they follow a traditional sequence of obligations of wives to husbands, children to parents, and slaves to masters. Such household patterns and metaphors carry us across the threshold into a world of culturally coded practices and institutions as well as legally enshrined relations foreign to modern notions of family and household.

Second, once we are alerted to these sets of codes, we are able to recognize important deviations from them as a consequence of social realities such as economics and religion. Greco-Roman tradition prescribed that women should marry young, obey their husbands, bear children, and not be seen in public. Household duties, especially those found in 1 Timothy 2:8–15 exhorting women to remain silent, learn from their husbands, and bear children, enshrine such ideas. However, Phoebe, Prisc(ill)a, Lydia, and possibly Nympha—businesswomen and artisans discussed in the last chapter—hardly conformed to these notions. They may be the biblical version of the enterprising women we see in surviving frescoes and reliefs selling goods from their shops (see Figure 5.1). Such portraits are instructive for imagining entrepreneurial women of the period, but perhaps more importantly they remind us that the poverty

FIGURE 5.1 Relief of Roman butcher shop, owner, and client, Rome, first century CE. Photo by author. Musea della civiltà Roma, Rome.

of most imperial residents would have made it impossible for the vast majority of urban women to remain sequestered at home and bearing children.

Further, religion sometimes played an important role in promoting deviance from traditional domestic roles. In a subtle but crucial way, the New Testament household codes, for example, transform a traditional hierarchical code by introducing a series of obligations that husbands have to their wives, parents to their children, and masters to their slaves. From our perspective such invocations are hardly revolutionary, but read against the backdrop of a strict, domestic hierarchical understanding, they are remarkable. A more dramatic departure can also be found in Paul's advice to the married—that due to the impending end of the world, they should "live as though they had no wives" (or husbands, one may assume; 1 Cor. 7:29). The questioning of household relations played an important role in shaping Christian behavior and belief in subsequent centuries. In the second-century *Acts of Paul and Thecla* (a writing that belongs to a body of literature collected under the general banner of *Apocryphal Acts of the Apostles*), the heroine of the story, a young, betrothed woman named Thecla, upon hearing the apostle preach, breaks off her engagement and dedicates herself to a life of virginity and discipleship, much to the consternation of her mother and fiancé.[1] Some argue that 1 Timothy's command that wives keep silent and bear children reflects resistance to the kinds of ideas one finds in Thecla's story, and that the letter was written to rein in women who were rejecting traditional arrangements as a consequence of being taught by Pauline teachers who "forbid marriage" (1 Tim. 4:3). Continence was a means of rejecting cultural codes and practicing a new identity. Christianity was one movement among many encouraging social experimentation by breaking away from traditional household codes.

Finally, the hierarchical nature of ancient domestic life invites us to consider the issue of perspective when interpreting ancient data. The household rules reflect the patriarchal organization of Greco-Roman society. That is, they reinforce the position of the male householder as husband, father, and—above all—master, and urge duties that preserve his authority. However, the New Testament also sometimes grants us access to ancient family life viewed from other perspectives. For example, the instructions to slaves in 1 Peter 2:18–25 describe situations where slaves are beaten even when they do right (v. 20), and thereby alert us to the brutality of ancient household life. Also, in 1 Corinthians 7:12–16, Paul instructs Christian wives that it is permitted to accept divorce from their unbelieving husbands, which offers a glimpse into possible tensions arising between partners who had differing religious beliefs. This raises the question of how the household looked from the underside of Greco-Roman households. In recent decades, scholars have given great attention to the lives of women, children, and slaves, and their experiences, in Greco-Roman and Jewish households. In doing so, they have brought into the light a multitude of people long shrouded by the darkness of patriarchal indifference.

PLACE, IDENTITY, AND PRACTICES

Archaeology furnishes us with a good understanding of the material conditions of family life in the ancient world. We know the most about the forms of the households of the Latin West, especially those from Pompeii and Herculaneum and their environs near the Bay of Naples, due to the fact of their almost perfect preservation in the ash from the eruption of Mount Vesuvius in 79 CE. Excavations of first-century aristocratic residences in Ephesus also furnish us with good knowledge of some wealthy eastern Mediterranean households. Alongside these, archaeological study of classical, Hellenistic, and imperial period houses from places such as Delos, Priene, Olynthos, and Pergamum offers further information on wealthier and more modest eastern Mediterranean residences. The innumerable *tabernae* or workshops of merchants found all across the empire are also instructive. Because of the several New Testament references to Christian artisans (many of which we took up in the last chapter), these *tabernae* are especially useful for imagining the living spaces of Jesus followers. The remains of *insulae* (apartment blocks), such as those found in the ancient port city of Ostia just outside Rome, furnish an understanding of the typical households and living conditions of the Empire's millions of non-elite urban residents in the capital.

In Pompeii and Herculaneum the residences of the wealthy, as well as some of the moderately affluent, took the form of "atrium houses." Such a house (*domus*—the word meant both "house" and "household") was organized around two or more courtyards (*atria*), which were open or partially open to the sky.

An elegant variation of the atrium was the peristyle (*peristylium*), a courtyard surrounded by a colonnade supporting the roof of a continuous covered porch—an arrangement repeated in the mediaeval cloister.

Each atrium was surrounded by a series of rooms (slaves' quarters, bedrooms, dining room(s), kitchen, storage facilities). The *domus* also contained one or more shrines for the worship of domestic gods. Rooms were elaborately decorated with floor mosaics and walls painted with geometrical patterns, mythological scenes, and/or landscapes, as well as figures to ward off evil and assure good fortune and fertility. The front atrium, which one could peer into from the street when the doors were opened each morning, contained the rooms where slaves typically slept and where, every morning, the male head of the household (paterfamilias) met his clients, received visitors, and gave daily instructions to his slaves. The rear courtyard was a more intimate space where the non-slave members of the family lived and where one or more dining rooms (*triclinia*) were often situated. Degrees of accessibility to these atria helped to inscribe status, as did other forms of organization, such as seating arrangements in the *triclinium*. At either side of the entrance, as well as around much of the household's perimeter, were a series of street-facing (usually rented) *tabernae*. Some atrium houses took the form of a more modest row house of two atria. More successful artisans owned a *domus* with street-facing *tabernae* lining one side of an atrium and accessible from it and some hypothesize that this is the kind of household more successful Christian merchants owned and where believers assembled for worship. The zones of accessibility of the Roman *domus* indicate that modern distinctions of private and public do not hold for these ancient households. *Domus* were busy places, prompting one Roman historian to describe them as "housefuls" rather than "households."[2]

The household (*oikos*) of the Greek East differed from that of the Latin West. The wealthier classical and Hellenistic *oikos* was a peristyle household organized around two juxtaposed courtyards, one modestly equipped, where the family typically lived, and the other more lavishly decorated for public activities such as the reception of guests, banquets, and symposia (after dinner speeches and discussion). The Roman architect and engineer Vitruvius (81 BCE–15 CE), describes the activities undertaken in each of these courtyards in gendered terms.[3] The less decorated one, the *gynaikonitis* or women's space, was for private domestic life; the other ornamented one, the *andronitis*, was the place for the male householder's public presentation and hence where the dining room, or *andron*, was located. Not all wealthy households took this form. Remains from third- to second-century BCE houses on the island of Delos and the city of Priene (40 kilometers south of Ephesus), as well as domestic structures from imperial Pergamum, are instructive, showing what typical modest houses and a few more lavish ones might have looked like and how they functioned. At Delos and Priene these were courtyard homes, so named because they were composed of an entrance into an elongated, paved courtyard, with living quarters at one end and storage rooms and a latrine at the other. In neither case were there double-courtyard homes of the type Vitruvius describes, nor is there material evidence of household spaces organized according to gender, although it is probable that the *gynaikonitis* was on the upper story and the *andron* on the ground floor. At Ephesus, excavation of a series of first-century hillside houses in the monumental heart of the city show rooms arranged around a peristyle courtyard, with living quarters on a second floor. *Tabernae* lined the front entrances at the foot of the hill. Archaeological remains of an *insula* from first-century Pergamum reveal a mixture of residences alongside each other, ranging from multiple-room atrium and peristyle houses to smaller single- or multiple-bedroom apartments. Street-facing *tabernae* ring the *insula* (see Figure 5.2).

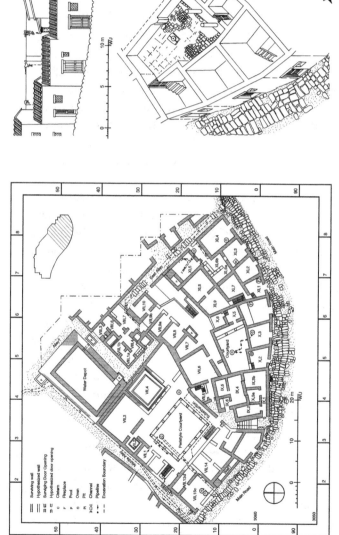

FIGURE 5.2 Ground plan, street view, and isometric drawing of *insula*, Pergamum, first third of second century CE. X,2,3,F (right) are *tabernae*. X,2 is a modest, two-story, courtyard house, possibly of a more prosperous artisan. Image created by author from sketches in Ulrike Wulf, *Die hellenistischen und römischen Wohnhäuser von Pergamon unter besonderer Berücksichtigung der Anlagen zwischen der Mittel und der Ostgasse. Altertümer von Pergamon Band XV. Die Stadtgrabung Teil 3* (Berlin: Walter DeGruyter, 1999), p. 206, Abb. 82 and p. 133, Abb. 67. Reproduced with permission of Ulrike Wulf.

Images created through geophysical archaeological methods suggest the harbor area of ancient Ephesus was made up of a tight network of similar *insulae*.

The last chapter discussed Roman and Ostian *insulae* as densely populated, multistory residential complexes consisting of a number of different types of dwellings, ranging from luxury apartments on the second floor to one-bedroom units on upper floors (see Figure 4.2). This was the chief means of housing the urban population in the capital. A fourth century CE record states there were 46,602 *insulae* and 1,797 *domus* in Rome. Apartment blocks were notorious for collapsing (Romans joked about the sound of them crashing down). Engineers lacked the knowledge necessary to design safe high-rise multi-occupancy dwellings and, to make things much worse, rapacious real-estate speculators employed the cheapest available labor and materials. Although Augustus and Nero tried to restrict the height of *insulae* to seven- and then six-story structures, they sometimes reached up to nine floors. The basic rule of thumb was that the higher one went, the poorer and more dangerous one's living quarters became. Virtually all of these spaces were rented, sometimes on a day-to-day basis. Beyond the third floor there was no plumbing; residents washed at public baths, and some relieved themselves in public latrines. Many, however, dumped their human waste together with their garbage through chutes onto the streets, a practice the city attempted in vain to restrict. There were neither heating nor cooking facilities on the upper floors, so residents prepared meals in the hallways on portable stoves. Rooms tended to be dark, since the only light that entered them was from the hallway. It has been argued that the series of greetings Paul extends to Roman Christians in Romans 16:3–16 should be understood as referring to groups of believers joined together in various assemblies meeting in *insulae* in different parts of the city.

A common feature across the empire was the *taberna* or workshop. *Tabernae*, again, are important for understanding the possible living conditions of first-century Christians because of the evidence that many were artisans. *Tabernae* typically took the form of a larger front room that served as the workshop and one or more chambers at the rear that simultaneously served as a residence, a place to store wares, and a production facility; alternatively, the shopkeeper and his or her family might occupy a mezzanine above the shop. In Pompeii there are several villas with rooms that open into *tabernae*. This suggests that the domestic economy of some households included workshops where slaves worked, or even that the entire household was engaged in workshop production. In single-room *tabernae* there was, of course, no distinction between the more public and private zones one finds in grander Greek and Roman households. We may ask how the many Christian artisans directly named or alluded to in the New Testament would have applied the exhortations of the hierarchical household codes to situations where families were piled into one-bedroom living spaces or were engaged in the economic production of workshops.

The question of what we can adduce from the household codes about the socioeconomic identity of early Christians brings us to the doorstep of a debate among scholars about where to situate the households of first-century Christians. Some argue that we should imagine them in elegant households, reclining at banquets in the *triclinium* or *andron*, transforming meals into Eucharistic celebrations, and symposia speeches (talks that often followed meals) into sermons. Others contend that they typically met in the mezzanines or at the back of *tabernae*. Still others make a case for meetings in rented spaces analogous to those where Greco-Roman associations met. The second-century Christian apologist Justin Martyr (100–165 CE) describes how he instructed Roman Christians in a rented room above a bath, and, intriguingly, he states that he is unaware of any other meetings of believers in the capital, a fact that can be readily accounted for by remembering that the people who lived in the densely populated city probably conducted most of their lives in and around their own insulae.[4] Again, as just alluded to, some look to the cramped one- or two-room apartments in the upper floor of an *insula* as the typical meeting place. That is the setting we can assume from Acts 20:9, which reports the death at Troas of the somewhat ironically named Eutychus ("Good Fortune"), who fell from a third-floor apartment window after falling asleep as Paul "talked on and on" at midnight (v. 11, NIV). One can also make a case for more upscale settings. In one passage Paul says of the Corinthians, "not many of you were wise by human standards, not many were powerful, not many were of noble birth" (1 Cor. 1:26). Many New Testament scholars infer from this that if "not many" were wealthy, some must have been. This has led to arguments that people like Phoebe, Stephanas, Lydia, Nympha, and Philemon lived in atrium houses and hosted Christians in their gardens, courtyards, and dining rooms. Most probably the settings of Christian assemblies differed from city to city. It is difficult to be persuaded by the argument that wealthy members typically patronized the Jesus movement. As we have seen, Paul counts himself among Christians who engaged in long hours of manual labor. Those who numbered themselves among the beneficiaries of the Roman economy, including those who, like Philemon, might own a slave, usually commanded only a modest degree of wealth. Like most urban dwellers, they lived in crowded quarters, and their livelihoods were subject to seasonal rhythms as well as the unpredictable weather patterns of the Mediterranean Basin. Taking these considerations into account, it seems safer to suppose that those Christians who found themselves in the atrium houses and luxury apartments of the more well to do were typically there as slaves and clients. It is notable that the household code of Colossians 3:18–4:1

dedicates the most words (vv. 22–25) to reasons slaves should obey their masters, and that the one found at 1 Peter 2:18–3.7 begins with instructions to slaves who are beaten by their unbelieving masters (2:18–25). Nevertheless, there is continuing debate concerning the diversity and socio-economic status of Christians in the Roman world.

MEN, WOMEN, AND GRECO-ROMAN HOUSEHOLDS

We turn now to a discussion of the people who populated the various dwellings of the period under consideration and the social and legal codes that shaped household relations. As most of the New Testament reflects social settings of the eastern Mediterranean, our chief focus will be on Greek families. To restrict the focus is important because of the multicultural aspects of imperial life. This means that while one can make general observations about households in this period, it is important to remember that there was no "one size fits all" code of family law and ethics. Nor can one generalize from what was true in Rome or the Latin West to the rest of the empire. For example, in 18–17 BCE, Augustus introduced a series of statutes promoting marriage and the bearing of children, while also punishing celibacy and childlessness after a certain age with restrictions on inheritances. Called the *leges Juliae* (named after the emperor's Julian family clan), they also legislated the remarriage of younger widows within ten months of a husband's death, prohibited adultery and sex outside of marriage, and forbade marriage between senators and freedpersons. In producing these laws, Augustus was partly motivated by a desire to promote his profile as a restorer of traditional values, which included advocating the growth and protection of the family. His chief aim, however, was to increase the population of the upper classes in Rome, whose numbers were diminishing due to increasing prosperity and decreasing birth rates, even as the capital swelled in size through immigration of slaves and foreigners.

While this was significant legislation for Roman elites, we should not assume it was applied or observed outside the capital and Roman colonies of the Greek East, let alone by non-elites. People across the empire lived in a variety of households. Many lived in informal arrangements as well as in mixed marriages (i.e., freedpersons with slaves). Some cities, such as Ephesus, Smyrna, and Athens, possessed special status that allowed them to pass their own laws. In general, outside Italy, Rome adapted its legislation to cohere with the statutes and customs developed over centuries in the Hellenistic states of the eastern Mediterranean. We may reasonably assume that generations of local customs resulted in idiosyncratic household rules and practices. For example, while Jewish families of the Diaspora did not differ significantly from Greek ones (they owned slaves, for example, and although the Bible sanctioned polygamy, they did not practice it), ritual observances such as circumcision, religious beliefs, and sacred texts had an important effect on the conduct of household life.

Roman law used two Latin words to designate the family and kinship: *domus* and *familia*. The term *domus* can be translated as "household. " It referred to the husband, wife, children, slaves, former slaves or freedpersons, clients, and other household residents. *Familia* signified a set of realities and meanings far different from the contemporary connotations associated with the English word "family." It designated cognates, or all blood relatives descended from a common male and female ancestor. It also referred to the agnates (i.e., those descended from a male ancestor) and the property under the legal authority (*patria potestas*, "paternal power") of the father or *pater* (the paterfamilias: pl. patresfamilias): his wife (materfamilias/matresfamilias), children, his sons' children, adopted children, unmarried daughters, and freedpersons, as well as animate (i.e., slaves and livestock) and inanimate property. Materially, *familia* denoted the property of a *domus* as well as that inherited from agnate and cognate kin.

The main responsibility of the paterfamilias was to preserve the *patrimonium*, the material conditions of the *familia*, intact for succeeding generations. His authority was enshrined by *patria potestas* (the legal power of a paterfamilias over his *familia*) and included the right of physical discipline of children and slaves, sexual exploitation of servants, and the life and death of newborns (see below). It was expected that fathers would exercise their *patria potestas* over children severely—they were to be as harsh with their children as masters were with their slaves, although legal license to torture slaves did not extend to children. Masters could also execute slaves; traditionally, although not exercised in the imperial period, *patria potestas* included the right of a father to punish disobedient sons and unchaste daughters with death. Paul evokes, albeit in an eastern Mediterranean context, the cultural meaning attached to disciplinary power of the paterfamilias when he likens life under the law to a child heir of an estate treated no better than a slave (Gal. 4:1–3). While admonishing the troubled and wayward Corinthian Christian assembly, he invokes patriarchal authority analogous to *patria potestas*, where he describes members "as beloved children," goes on to portray himself as their "father in Christ Jesus through the Gospel" (1 Cor. 4:14, 15), and then threatens to discipline them "with a stick" (v. 21).

Although the title materfamilias is analogous to paterfamilias, a matron did not exercise *patria potestas* over her husband's property. She did, however, exercise sole authority over any *patrimonium* inherited from her father, which could afford her a degree of independence from her husband. The word materfamilias implied a set of virtues that were to guide a wife's conduct in the management of her household. Together with all the subordinates of the household, *pietas*—a term one ancient Roman historian describes as "reciprocal, dutiful affection"—shaped her relationship with the paterfamilias.[5] *Patria potestas* and *pietas* bound household members together. As we will see when we turn to a discussion of the self, a number of gender- and status-specific virtues seen as prescribed by nature and the gods shaped how householders, wives, masters, and slaves were to behave toward one another.

Greek uses two words for household, *oikos* and *oikia*, terms that correspond to the Latin terms *domus* and *familia*, but without the same precision. Like their counterparts, they designated the property and persons of a household, including the slaves, freedpersons, and extended kin of a patrilineal estate. Thus, *Caesari familia*, the household of Caesar, which refers to the emperor's slaves and freedpersons occupied in the imperial administration, is usually rendered *Kaisaros oikos/oikia* in Greek (for example, Philippians 4:22 refers to "the emperor's household [*oikos*]"). We can see Paul using this wider sense when he celebrates the devotion of the household (*oikia*) of Stephanas for its service to the apostle's mission (1 Cor. 16:15), or when the Pastoral Epistles use the same word, *oikia*, to refer to female household members influenced by itinerant teachers as well as household property (1 Tim. 5:13; 2 Tim. 2:20; 3.6; also 2 John 10). When Paul refers to the baptism of Stephanas's household (*oikos*) in 1 Corinthians 1:16, this probably means all of its members. Similar connotations are implied in a variety of New Testament references to believers and their households (Acts 10:2; 16:15; 16:31, 34; 18:8; 2 Tim. 1:16; 3:6; 2 Tim. 1:16; 4:19; Titus 2:5). Paul refers to baptizing the synagogue ruler, Crispus (1 Cor. 1:14) and Acts 18.8 portrays him becoming a believer "together with all his household [*oikō*]." In his letter to Philemon we see Paul similarly working with Greek notions of the family as *oikos*. In it, the apostle corresponds with Philemon concerning his slave Onesimus. Paul describes how he received a slave but sent him home as Philemon's brother—perhaps a reference to his conversion while with Paul (Philem. 10, 15–16). Most scholars have interpreted the letter as an attempt to urge Philemon to have mercy on his fugitive slave. However, some have argued recently that it is not about how a master is to receive a runaway slave, but rather a request that he either free his slave or loan him to Paul for his Gospel mission. In either case, the letter is a masterpiece of diplomacy whereby an apostle exercises a divinely conferred authority over a Christian believer and subtly seeks to redefine the relationship between a master and his human property: no longer master and slave, but brothers, and both children of their spiritual father, the apostle. At the same time, it is a case study in a master's legal power over his slave and how far ancient understandings of household and family are from modern Western ones.

There are no Greek words for paterfamilias, materfamilias, or *patria potestas*, but the Greek terms *kyrios/a* (lord, master) and *oikodespotēs* (householder) are rough equivalents. We can see this in New Testament usage. There, *kyrios/a* appears repeatedly to refer to male/female household authority, often of a master over his slave and/or estate (Matt. 6:24; Mark 13:35; Luke 14:21–23; John 15:15, 20; Eph. 6:5, 9; Col. 4:1; also 2 John 1, 5). The term, *oikodespotēs*, also appears frequently in the Gospels and is usually translated "householder" or "landowner" in the NRSV (Matt. 13:27, 52; Mark 14:14; Luke 22:11). In 1 Timothy 5.14, Paul outlines a set of duties analogous to those of the Roman materfamilias when he exhorts young widows "to marry, bear children and govern their households [*oikodespotein*]." Outside the Gospels, the household rules referred to above identify the responsibilities of a male householder and those under his authority in ways that are very similar to Roman expectations concerning patresfamilias and their *familiae*. By the time New Testament writers developed them, centuries of use made them commonplace. In Greek literature they formed part of a larger theme of household or estate governance, *oikonomia* (whence we get the English word "economy"). Aristotle (384–322 BCE) reflects their patriarchal orientation when he defines the city-state as an assembly of households and then goes on to describe a *kyrios*'s correct management of his wife, children, slaves, and property as indispensable for the right functioning of the polis.[6] The *kyrios*, he argues, has three roles: husband, father, and master. The larger social expectation of the *kyrios* was similar to that defined for a paterfamilias: to preserve and promote the interests of his household through self-restraint and right use of authority. The household was the place where masculine identity was crafted and power exerted through self-discipline and control of others, whether it took the form of sexual domination of wives and slaves, corporal punishment of servants, or the strict punishment of children. The household codes of Colossians and Ephesians are remarkable for how they presumably restrict these kinds of practices by listing reciprocal obligations of husbands, fathers, and masters to the rest of the household.

In the traditional Greek and early Hellenistic household, the ideal wife was not seen or heard in public and confined herself to gender-specific zones of the *oikos*: the hearth, places for the production of household necessities such as weaving, and the bedroom. The *andron* (dining room), as the name implies, was a domain restricted to men and their friends. A wife's domestic tasks included attending to daily religious rites for the protection of her house, the rudimentary education of her children, and burial rituals. But they also entailed the management of the internal life of an *oikos*. Although written in the fourth century BCE, the treatise *Oeconomicus* (*On Household Management*), by the philosopher Xenophon (431–354 BCE), outlines the tasks and duties of a wife. The document takes the form of a dialogue in which Socrates describes how a householder named Ischomachus taught his young teenage wife to manage his estate's household budget, as well as its slaves and domestic production, and even what clothes to set out for him when he went out in public. He also relates how he trained her to control her passions, especially her speech, so as to assure his house was properly regulated and did not bring him public shame.[7] A series of documents written perhaps as late as the third century BCE, purporting to be letters written by noteworthy women following the philosophy of Pythagoras to female protégés, outlines similar domestic duties and behaviors. The documents include a letter from Theano to Kallisto on how a young wife should manage domestic slaves, and another from Melissa to Kleareta on how to be a good and faithful wife.[8] Although they present themselves as from women, and some scholars treat them as such, there is good reason to think men penned them and used pseudonyms to promote their domestic interests. The Pastoral Epistles echo these Pythagorean ideals when they advise women to be silent, modestly adorned, self-controlled, obedient to their husbands, and faithful mothers.

The Pastorals also reflect the broader political view that orderly households create good societies. The writer depicts the church as "the household of God" (1 Tim. 3:15); its correct functioning depends on the proper behavior of the families comprising it. Ecclesial leaders are the "chamberlains" (*oikonomoi*, see below) of their master's *oikos* (Titus 1:7). As such, they can only govern if they prove themselves worthy of the important task their heavenly householder has entrusted to them; that is, if they rule their households properly—namely by regulating both themselves and those under them, especially their wives and children (1 Tim. 3:4–6; Titus 1:6–9). They should teach their wives at home (1 Tim. 2:11–12). Fathers are "to keep their children submissive and respectful in every way" (1 Tim. 3:4). Furthermore, "younger widows" (*chērai*, a Greek term that can refer to both single young and widowed women)—that is, the majority of the assembly's women given the average life expectancy of males—should (re)marry and exercise the roles of wife and mother and the tasks of governing their households (1 Tim.

5:11–14). Even "real widows" (defined as over sixty in 1 Tim. 5:9—of whom there would have been very few) are to engage in a traditional round of duties culturally prescribed for them, including the instruction of children and grandchildren (1 Tim. 5:4). While slaves are not expressly mentioned, it is probable that they are implied in the prescriptions of 1 Timothy 3:4–6 and Titus 1:5–9. In other words, these are classic applications of the household *topos*, with nothing to suggest reciprocal obligations of *kyrioi* to their subordinates.

The Pastorals rehearse traditional household virtues in part to rein in women, specifically widows who, the Pastor complains, go out in public from household to household and do not marry or (re)marry (1 Tim. 5:11–13). Perhaps the amount of attention given to trying to curtail such activities reflects the independence of Roman imperial women. For example, they had the right to initiate divorce and own and manage property, as did women in the Greek East. Paul confirms this when advises Christian women not to divorce an unbelieving husband if he consents to live with her (1 Cor. 7:13–14). When he refers to the assembly of Christians at Laodicea who meet in Nympha's house (Col. 4:15), we should imagine a woman who owns and controls property, just as we should when we hear Paul describe Phoebe as the patron of both him and the church at Cenchreae (Rom. 16:1–2). These women hardly conform to the traditional ideals set out for Christian women in 1 Timothy. Further, in the period under consideration, women of the eastern Mediterranean were exercising both public and private roles that went beyond what one might otherwise expect from the household codes. Wealthier women were hosting and attending banquets, reclining on benches beside their husbands, and giving speeches at symposia traditionally restricted to men. They owned slaves and ran businesses. While they did not hold elected office, they held priesthoods and other honorific posts. Given the lower economic status of Christians, one should be careful imagining that Jesus believers were doing the same. Nevertheless, names of women who were not domiciled wives but were exercising important roles of leadership in Christian assemblies abound in the New Testament: Prisc(ill)a and Aquila are patrons of house churches (1 Cor. 16:19; see Rom. 16:3; also Acts 18:1–3); and Paul names Junia as a co-apostle with Andronicus (Rom. 16:7). He implies important tasks of service when he describes Mary, Tryphaena, and Tryphosa as workers among Roman Christians (Rom. 16:6, 12); "worker" is a term he uses to describe his own activities as well as those of patrons (e.g., 1 Cor. 15:10; 16:16; Gal. 4:11; Phil. 2:16; 1 Thess. 1:3; 3:5; 5:12; see also 1 Tim. 5:17). He also names Philologos and Julia (Rom. 16.15), perhaps a married couple promoting Paul's Gospel. Arguably, Paul's eschatological focus on a new order where old distinctions of ethnicity, status, and gender have been swept away furnished Christians religious warrants to practice the kinds of social innovations unfolding in their larger social contexts.

Paul was not alone in promoting these ideals of shared work and mutual care. One modern historian has described what she identifies as "the sentimental ideal of the Roman family" in the early empire.[9] Grave reliefs, for example, regularly portrayed wives and children in scenes of family love and devotion, and described the deceased with inscriptions celebrating the fatherly or motherly virtues of the departed and the close emotional bonds between spouses and children (see Figure 5.3).

One also discovers the same patterns in literary culture. A treatise by Plutarch instructs a young bride and groom to love one another and unite in philosophical contemplation.[10] Plutarch is addressing an elite couple who could afford to pay for grave reliefs featuring domestic bliss and clearly were people of some means. Nevertheless, the values extolled are those embodied in the household codes. On the ground, perhaps the relation of Prisca and Aquila is most telling of what was more typical of artisan urban dwellers who were also Christians: they

FIGURE 5.3 Funerary monument of an artisan, Pergamum, early Roman period. The inscription reads, "Hephaestion son of Papas farewell." Lower left, Hephaestion is portrayed at work. His spouse sits before her departed husband and Papas reclining at a banquet. The smaller figures are slave attendants. Photo by author. Istanbul Archaeological Museum, Turkey.

work alongside each other as "tentmakers" or weavers and act as hosts to assemblies. Did the married partners Andronicus and Junia or Philologos and Julia do the same as they labored for Paul's Gospel? That we cannot know, but it is certain that whatever legal provisions and cultural traditions dictated household relations, practical necessities of material survival encouraged a life of shared work.

CHILDREN

The United Nations Convention on the Rights of the Child defines a child as any person under the age of eighteen unless otherwise specified by national law, and it outlines a series of rights that include physical and emotional security, healthcare, education, legal protection, and freedom from sexual and physical exploitation and gender discrimination.[11] Children in ancient households had none of these rights. *Patria potestas* gave fathers the right to flog, imprison, and even kill disobedient children. Alongside this, it was commonplace across the empire to kill, sell, or expose unwanted children. *Patria potestas* accorded the paterfamilias the right to refuse entry of a newborn into its *familia* until its naming ceremony, eight or nine days after birth. Fathers exercised the same right in the Greek East. Practices of infanticide, exposure (*expositio*), and the selling of children were usually motivated by economic considerations; babies born with deformities or disabilities were often killed. Romans and Greeks deposited exposed infants in public places such as doorsteps, temples, crossroads, or rubbish heaps, where they would perish or, more likely, be collected by agents who would sell them into slavery. Sometimes they were found and raised by household slaves, or they might be taken into homes and absorbed as members of the *familia*. Jews did not practice exposure, which Greeks and Romans considered odd. Philo decried it as "a very ordinary piece of wickedness among other nations by reason of their natural inhumanity," an opinion echoed by other contemporary Jews.[12]

Alongside foundlings were poor freeborn children abandoned due to the death of parents or given up for financial reasons to another family who could care for them. With rates of infant mortality as high as they were (arguably, half of all children died before the age of two), parents needed to conceive five to seven children to assure surviving heirs and material support in their old age. However, in poor families, three children at most could be supported. As the ancient world had no social services for the care of unwanted children, they either died or were raised in other households. There is evidence that circulation of foster children (called *alumni* in Latin and *threptoi* in Greek) was a widespread practice in the ancient world. There are few records about these children, but the surviving evidence indicates that they became manual laborers as soon as possible and that they were chronically malnourished. The situation was different when a slave gave birth. Her child (called a *verna*) was the property of her master and could be sold at will, although there is evidence that *vernae* often had a special status in *familiae*, were treated affectionately, and grew up with their masters' children.

This grim picture is offset by a surprising celebration of children in surviving material and written sources. In imperial iconography, for example, children appear frequently. A panegyric treatise to the emperor Trajan by Pliny the Younger remembers mothers and children who flocked to Rome in gratitude of the emperor's policies dedicated to their care. Pliny writes, "You [Trajan] are a prince whose reign makes it both a pleasure and profit to rear children."[13] He likens his rule to that of "a father living with his children" and throughout his treatise he calls the emperor "parent," "our parent," and even "common parent of us all."[14] An arch at Benevento in Italy, celebrating the emperor

Trajan's *alimenta* (food donations) for boys up to eighteen and girls up to fourteen, depicts a number of young children. Around a table on which the grain donation is placed, a mother holds her infant, children sit on their fathers' shoulders, and boys and girls hold the hands of their parents. A similar spirit is evident in grave monuments representing sons and daughters alongside portraits of the surviving partner mourning or engaging in a ritual commemoration.

Biblical texts reflect these currents. Even as the New Testament household codes urge children to be obedient to their parents, it instructs parents not to provoke them (Eph. 6:1, 4; Col. 3:20–21). In a treatise outlining how children should be educated, Plutarch observes that severe punishment of children is counterproductive and that praise and reproof should be used in equal measure: "[I]t is well to choose some time when the children are full of confidence rather than to put them to shame by rebuke, and then in turn to cheer them up by praises."[15] Titus instructs "young women to love their husbands, to love their children" (Titus 2:4). In 2 Timothy 1:5 the author celebrates the close bonds Timothy had with his grandmother Lois and his mother, Eunice. The New Testament consistently depicts believers as children living under the care and discipline of their loving, divine father.

We know most about children raised in elite Roman households. The birth took place at home with the help of a midwife, often in the company of other female family members. Religious rituals—prayers as well as superstitious practices—accompanied every stage of procreation: conception, gestation, birth, and postnatal care. In Roman households, after the paterfamilias made the decision to accept the child into the *familia*, a male baby was named after nine days (a female, eight days later) at a special ceremony, the *lustratio*. In the Greek East, the naming ceremony occurred between five and ten days after birth. As in Rome, until that day, children had no legal existence and could be exposed. On the day of the name-giving cere-mony, or a day or more before it, the baby was carried around the hearth and physically inspected, followed by sacrifice and feasting in the company of relatives and friends, who brought birthday gifts.

Jewish male children were named eight days after birth, at their circumcision; girls may have been named at analogous ceremonies (perhaps immersion), though of course without cir-cumcision, a nonpractice that receives much attention in early rabbinic literature. We know remarkably little about the lives of Jewish children in the Roman Empire. Echoing the Bible, first-century authors like Philo placed a heavy emphasis, particularly for males, on education in Jewish law and tradition, and for girls on being shaped for domestic responsibilities.

In elite households of both the East and West, wet nurses nourished infants and for three months to three years after they were weaned continued as their companions. Alongside the wet nurse were a variety of other slave helpers. Sometimes a male slave, called a *nutritor* or *nutricius*, also took part in the feeding and comforting of children, as well as reading to them and rocking them to sleep. It is possible that Paul portrays him-self in this role when he tells the Corinthians he fed them "with milk not solid food" (1 Cor. 3:1–2).

In these same households, both sexes were educated. Among the other slaves who cared for the children, the most impor-tant was the *paedagōgos*, whose task was to take the children to and from school, supervise them, and attend to their moral formation. Instruction focused on the three R's, accompanied by a heavy dose of physical punishment. It is this image Paul invokes when he likens the Law to a *paedagōgos* who disciplines a freeborn child until maturity in Galatians 3:24, and where he draws a sharp contrast between himself and others: "For though you might have ten thousand guardians [*paedagōgoi*] in Christ, you do not have many fathers. Indeed, in Christ Jesus I became your father through the gospel" (1 Cor. 4:15). Education typically took the form of dictating, memorizing, and reciting from a list of set Greek and Latin texts. The chief aim of education was to socialize, not to inform or help students learn to think independently. *Paedagōgoi* were generally well educated, which set them apart from the teachers in the schools, who were often of low status, were poorly paid, and whose sole job was to drill the contents of traditional texts into their charges for the purpose of rote learning. If they offered any (reliable) commentary, it was based on whatever information they may have independently gleaned concerning the topics being taught, which explains why elite Italian families sent their children to reputable centers of learning like Athens. No one went to school to learn to be a teacher. Slave children could be taught by their parents or educated fellow slaves; *vernae* often attended school with their freeborn siblings. Imperial slaves had the benefit of imperial schools, where they gained instruction for their work in the administration.

Child slaves and children of free and freed artisans faced a different reality. They were seen as important assets and were trained to realize the greatest economic gain for the household. They began working at various tasks when they were still young children. Across the empire, adulthood was usually fixed, as it was in Rome, at fourteen years. By that age, if not earlier, masters and parents expected boys to be fully occupied in whatever form of production they were trained to perform. Male children as young as nine years old began to learn whatever skills would contribute to the household economy. Masters sometimes trained their child slaves in order to make them more valuable when sold. There is good evidence that as a means of diversifying the domestic economy, a father often encouraged his son to train in a trade different from his own and to set up an independent shop. Where fathers and sons worked in the same trade, they often worked in separate shops. Apprenticeships prepared children for the long hours of work that awaited them for the remainder of their lives; some references describe them working from sunrise to sundown. Girls were usually married in their early teens, between the ages of twelve and sixteen, and were prepared by their mothers for their coming domestic duties. In Titus 2:3–5 the Pastor advises older women to teach younger women "to love their husbands, to love their children, to be self-controlled, chaste, good managers of the household, kind, being submissive to their husbands, so that the word of God may not be discredited." In more well-off households (as the passage from Xenophon cited above indicates) duties might include stewardship of resources and the supervision of slaves, as well as whatever other skills advanced the family's livelihood. Female slaves were trained for specific tasks. As in elite households, boys and girls learned from their father or mother the round of domestic religious observances to preserve the family's well-being.

In the case of the Jewish Diaspora, it has been argued that some important differences from Roman views on how children should be valued and treated resulted from a long written and oral sacred tradition that celebrated children as the sign of God's blessing and the fulfillment of God's promises to Abraham's posterity. We have already referred to a rejection of infant exposure. The Hebrew Bible's emphasis on learning and contemplating the Torah (Deut. 5:1; 17:19; 31:12; Josh. 1:8; Ps. 1:2; 119:48; Isa. 34:16; see Luke 4:16) has led to the idea that Jewish rates of literacy were higher than in the general population (often probably too conservatively calculated at 10–15%, although greater in cities) and that parents were motivated to teach their children to read. Josephus defends his religion by arguing that Jewish children are taught to read so that from earliest childhood they may follow Israel's traditions.[16] This is important for estimating the literacy of children of Jewish Christians, as well as their ability to follow and understand the uses of the

Scriptures. In 2 Timothy 3:15, the Pastor celebrates his protégé Timothy: "[F]rom childhood you have known the sacred writings that are able to instruct you for salvation through faith in Christ Jesus."

SLAVES AND FREEDPERSONS

It is conservatively estimated that slaves constituted 10% of the population of the Roman Empire. One-third of them lived in Italy, and some calculate that slaves and freedpersons constituted as many as two-thirds of the capital's residents. The rest were unevenly distributed across the empire, mostly on agricultural estates and in mines. Although conquest had historically supplied Rome and its empire with slaves, by the first century most were furnished through slave reproduction, slave dealers collecting exposed infants, and poverty-stricken people voluntarily selling themselves in order to gain material security. Apart from cruelty and brutality, slavery in the ancient world was different from that of the antebellum American South, as well as from how popular entertainment typically portrays it, where there is often a focus on slave uprisings and attempted revolution. There were certainly slave revolts in the Roman world, but these were in the centuries prior to the Common Era. Furthermore, few questioned the institution of slavery, as it was seen as a part of the natural order and indispensable for the functioning of the domestic and imperial economy. The fact that New Testament authors nowhere condemn slavery but rather assume its continuation does not mean that biblical writers were "conservatives" or were committed to the perpetuation of injustice. Slavery was so integral a part of the fabric of Roman, Greek, and Jewish society that they simply took it for granted. Against this backdrop, Paul's statement that in Christ "there is no longer slave or free" (Gal. 3:28) is remarkable, as are the instructions to masters to treat their slaves "justly and fairly, for you know that you also have a Master in heaven" (Col. 4:1).

Slaves across the Roman Empire could be used as their masters wished. The instruction in Ephesians 6:5 that slaves should obey their owners with "fear and trembling" speaks to the threat of abuse and violence in the treatment of slaves, as does the depiction in 1 Peter 2:18–24, where the words "harsh," "endure pain," "suffering unjustly," "beaten," and "abused" appear in quick succession, together with the analogy of Christ's crucifixion. Ancient literature is filled with references to the mistreatment of slaves, especially their use as sex objects. Slave dealers often castrated boys for sale as sex objects, girls were bought to generate income through prostitution, children were purchased solely for the sake of sexual gratification, and so on. Because there was no fear of pregnancy, enslaved wet nurses were often candidates for sexual exploitation. While some of these practices, such as the castration of boys, were considered illegal, it was not because of notions of compassion or justice. So far as sex was concerned, the right of a dominant party to penetrate a subordinate was considered natural. As for physical punishment, this was the prerogative of a master, limited only by the dictates of his or her conscience. Disobedient slaves were regularly made a public example. Flogging and beating were commonplace; in order to ensure obedience, disobedience by one slave might result in punishment for the entire household of servants. In some places, masters could rent devices for torturing their slaves, including tools for crucifixion. All of this helped to instill a continual fear of punishment, a state often championed as a means of social control. "Stop threatening them [slaves]," exhorts Ephesians 6:9.

In spite of all that, some slaves were treated remarkably well. While threats and violence were an inducement to work hard, intelligent masters knew that poorly treated slaves could be dangerous and unproductive. They were also a costly investment. At the low end, we have a record of the sale of a seven-year-old girl for 200 denarii (i.e., two-thirds of an annual wage for a soldier or unskilled laborer); at the upper limit there is a bill of sale for 700,000 sesterces (175,000 denarii). Alongside this, masters needed to clothe, house, and feed their slaves. It was hardly in their best interest to destroy their property. Thus, the opposite of the grim treatments discussed above also took place. Masters rewarded good service to foster obedience. The most cherished prize was freedom, which will be discussed in further detail below. They gave their slaves time to be with their partners and children and allowed them to take holidays on days of the calendar traditionally set aside specifically for them (the *Saturnalia* [17–23 December] and *Compitalia* [3–5 January]). Sometimes they treated them as confidants, left them a share of their inheritance or *patrimonium*, fell in love with them, and even set them free in order to marry them. The ideal master-slave relationship was one marked by *pietas*, loyalty (*fides*), and obedience (*obsequium*). Both parties had an interest in nurturing a good relationship, which helps to explain the reason there were not widespread slave insurrections during the period under discussion.

Slavery resulted in complex household arrangements. Masters owned the children their slaves conceived, and could separate them from their mothers to sell them. This is the backdrop to Paul's allegorical treatment of Hagar and Sarah in Galatians 4:22–31; the former is a domestic slave who bears children for slavery (v. 24), while Sarah's children are born for freedom (v. 23). Similarly, although domestic slaves could become couples and be married in all but name, masters were under no obligation to keep them together. There are several instances where a slave once freed purchased his or her partner or children from a master. In Pompeii and Rome there were typically more male than female slaves, which meant that when slaves fell in love they often belonged to different households.

The long-term viability of such relationships was fragile. On the other hand, there were mixed unions between a master and a slave, or a freedperson and a slave, or even a freeborn person and a freedperson. This could result in legal complexities. The rule of thumb for children of mixed relations was that they received the status the mother had when they were born. While masters regularly had sexual relations with their slaves, they could not marry them, as Roman law forbade marriage between people of unequal status, including between the freeborn and the freed. Roman law described the monogamous relationship between two people of unequal status (a paterfamilias with a freedperson of another *familia* or between a freed and freeperson) as concubinage or *contubernalis*. Unless adopted by their father, children produced by a paterfamilias with his concubine were illegitimate. We can expect that these restrictions simply resulted in many types of informal relationships.

Slaves in both the West and the East could hope to receive or purchase manumission (freedom). Paul refers to this institution when he instructs Christian slaves to take advantage of any opportunity to receive their freedom (1 Cor. 7:21). The institutions connected with manumission were different in the western and the eastern Mediterranean. In the West, depending on the type of manumission one received, a male/female freedperson (*libertus/a*; pl. *liberti/ae*) could remain part of the *pater*'s *familia* and under his *patria potestas*, and formally received the master's name. For example, when Tiro, a slave of the Roman rhetorician and consul Cicero (106–43 CE), became a *libertus*, he was named Marcus Tullius M. l(ibertus) Tiro. Before this he was simply Marci s(ervus) or Marci. Another option was to use the name of the master's *nomen* or *gens* as shorthand. This is potentially instructive for identifying the social origins of several Christians named by Paul in the greetings list of Romans 16. It is possible that Junia (v. 7), Herodion (11), and Julia (15) were (children of) freedpersons whose names reflect their connections with the *gentilica* (noble) names of the Julian, Junian, and Herodion clans. Adopting the names of a master designated a lifelong obligation of *fides* (loyalty) to him or her and, in the case of a *gentilicum*, conferred status.

   Manumission was regulated and created new household relationships and obligations. In the West, Roman law stated that slaves could not be manumitted before age thirty, and only by masters older than twenty. It specified two types of manumission, one granting a freedperson citizenship, and the other not. The former depended on a number of things, the most important of which was whether a slave had ever been shackled, found guilty of theft or immorality, or taken part in particular kinds of professions—a critical point, since slaves were often employed by their masters in a variety of activities. The twenty-year age limit was a means of assuring that the master offering freedom had the maturity and discernment to do so. The thirty-year limit implied long waits for manumission, and, given early mortality, many did not live that long. However, there were exceptions that made it possible to receive it earlier. First, slaves could hope to receive testamentary manumission, or freedom upon the master's death, which might also include receiving money or property as well as continuing inclusion in the *familia*. Second, if they worked in certain occupations, such as being a *paedagōgos*, or were of a specific status, such as being a *verna*, they could legally be manumitted when the master wished. Third, masters and freedpersons could form informal relationships that were manumission in all but name. These last two forms of freedom were based on *beneficium*; that is, as a reward for good service. In both cases, freedpersons moved from a master-slave relationship to a patron-client one, from being property to being a part of the *familia*, subject to *patria potestas*. This meant the continuation of a relationship between former slaves and freedpersons that was mutually beneficial; it was for this reason that it was the preferred form. For example, because they were part of the *familia*, the cremated remains of such persons could be placed in the family tomb or columbarium, where an inscription would identify their free status and sometimes their virtues. Freedpersons of elite households sometimes continued to live in the master's household, doing the same tasks they had done before they were manumitted. They could even live within the same *domus* with their own slaves. Or, they received a place to live with other clients of the same *familia*. They were also entitled to a daily allotment of grain or money. On the other hand, manumission meant that freedpersons had obligations of service (called *operae*) to the paterfamilias. This helped to preserve the patron-client relationship that guided many social relationships in the wider society. *Operae* might include conceiving a child as a replacement slave, giving a portion of income generated through the *peculium* (see below), managing a master's business or a sum of money given for investment, undertaking a journey for a master, and so on.

As freedpersons were now members of the *familia*, this included a lifelong duty of *fides* (loyalty) and *obsequium* (deference). This could imply a requirement to live near the paterfamilias or a need for permission to move residence to another city. In some cases we can imagine cells, or even *insulae*, of freedpersons and their families living in the neighborhood of their paterfamilias. Generally, we should imagine neighborhoods or networks of masters, slaves, freedpersons, and free persons arranged around a wealthy household. *Tabernae* in such neighborhoods might be the shops of freedpersons lining the master's residence or situated below a luxury apartment. In such circumstances Christianity might have spread rapidly through neighborhoods where the institutions of slavery and manumission had created dense webs of social contacts within densely packed populations.

One other means of gaining freedom was to purchase it, which usually entailed paying the amount it took to replace oneself. This severed the relationship between the master and the freedperson. Purchase often occurred when a partner or parent paid for their *contubernalis* or *verna*.

As an incentive to good work and the possibility of purchasing freedom, some masters gave their slaves an allowance (*peculium*) and allowed them to earn money through their work. The *peculium*, which in elite households could also include large amounts of capital that the slave could help grow through business dealings, was usually left to a freedperson upon manumission. For example, many slaves engaged in trades for their owners, for which they were paid wages or took a share of the profits. Wealthy masters regularly entrusted their slaves with funds to make money on their behalf (a situation the New Testament Parable of the Talents [Luke 19:12–27; Matt. 25:14–30] describes) as well as management of significant wealth and oversight of a large staff of the enslaved household. Sometimes manumission did not change these duties but transferred them as constituent portions of the patron-client relationship. In some cases, large *peculia* allowed slaves to ease their burden through the purchase of under-slaves (*vicarii*); it also gave slaves the means to amass considerable fortunes that included their own large residences. In the case of manumission, freedpersons sometimes continued to live in the households of their patrons with their under-slaves. Thanks to their training in business dealings and shrewd financial dealings with money entrusted to them, some freedpersons made considerable wealth in the Roman imperial economy. Some of them built their own tombs and imitated their former owners by depicting themselves iconographically as self-regulated and virtuous. The nouveau riche, gauche, freedperson wannabe was a favorite butt of Roman satire.[17] In some New Testament scholarship a great deal is made of these figures, and it has been argued that Christianity compensated for the "status inconsistency" that arose from freedpersons amassing riches without status.[18] It is worth remembering that such people constituted a small fraction of the imperial population.

In the East, manumission (there is no single Greek word that corresponds to the Latin *manumissio*) involved different procedures that had developed independently from place to place, over several centuries. Some generalizations are possible. A slave usually negotiated with the master over what it would cost to replace him, which often resulted in inflated prices. Manumission could be unconditional or conditional, and it could include some or all of the following: the right to act as one's own legal person, to pursue one's own occupation, to live wherever one wished, and to be free from seizure of property. All manumission included the first right. The unconditional form involved all four and was accordingly far more expensive. Conditional manumission implied continuing obligations or *operae* to the master. These were often exploitative arrangements wherein the manumitted effectively remained a slave in all but name. Unlike Roman slaves, those in the East could own property, take on second jobs, and enter into loans or business arrangements with others in order to raise the capital to pay for their freedom. Also different from the West, there were no regulations determining the minimum age for manumission. Unlike Rome, where manumission could also bring enrolment as a citizen, in the Greek East an unconditionally freed slave was enrolled as a metic (i.e., with the status of a resident alien). Unlike the West, there were no naming conventions upon being freed. It is interesting to speculate what range of obligations Paul had in mind when he described Christians as freedpersons (*apeleutheroi*) of the Lord (1 Cor. 7:22).

THE DEAD

In the secular West, there is a pervasive attempt to deny death and keep it from public view. Increasingly, those who die ask the bereaved not to conduct a funeral or other commemoration. There was no such denial in the ancient world, where high rates of mortality were the rule, and one could hardly be shielded from death. Deceased relatives were regularly commemorated on special days, such as the anniversary of the death or on days set aside when all of society remembered the deceased. Other festivals were designed to ward off threats from the restless dead.

Romans and Greeks had paradoxical views of the afterlife. On the one hand, they gathered to commemorate the dead as though they were present at certain ritual celebrations, which we will consider directly. On the other hand, although there was a general idea of the afterlife, there was no clear picture of it, and it is debated how common such belief was. It was widely held that a remarkable few—heroes and heroines who were distinguished by special qualities such as power, charisma, military or political achievement, or even exceptional beauty—continued to have a powerful existence after death, enjoying life in Elysium and the Isles of the Blessed. The rest of the unremarkable departed, which is to say just about everybody, were thought to live a shadow-like existence in Hades. The latter view is captured well by the Epicurean tomb inscription *Non fui, fui, non sum, non curo* (I was not, I was, I am not, I do not care). The fact that this epitaph is often found widely in abbreviated form (NFFNSNC) on tombstones attests its popularity beyond Epicurean circles. This leads one to think that people's thoughts about what one could expect after death and about the state of the dead were, like everything else in the ancient world, status-specific and dependent on context and occasion.

Burial customs differed in the West and East. In the West, prior to the Common Era, the dead were cremated and their ashes placed in urns and then buried or deposited in large columbaria, or placed in underground chambers (*hypogea*), in rectangular niches (*loculi*) cut into the walls of catacombs, or in walled enclosures of several tombs open to the sky. As we have seen, membership in a *familia* meant the right of having one's ashes in a family tomb; the ashes of slaves might also be placed there, as several epitaphs commissioned by *contubernales* indicate. In the Greek East, the deceased were buried. Among Jews and Christians, burial rather than cremation was the norm, perhaps motivated in part by belief in the resurrection of the body, a notion that was regularly derided by Christianity's opponents.

Funerary and ancestral rituals are often a means of marking the passage of the dead into the afterlife and preserving a fruitful relationship between the two realms. Every death threatens the social order and its continuation; one of the ways that threat is symbolized culturally is by conceiving the dead as potentially dangerous. In our death-denying society, horror movies attest to the fact that the continuing threat of death and the disorder it represents cannot be wished away. After twelve movie sequels, the slasher Jason of *Friday the 13th* appears to be particularly indestructible.

Rituals of mourning and burial were important rites of passage in antiquity that assured the deceased reached their final destination and did not mix into the affairs of the living. In both the East and the West, a continuing relationship with the dead was secured by commemorating them at a special meal at the graveside (called a *refrigerium* by the Romans). Iconographical representations of funerary banquets suggest that women had the primary responsibility for hosting these meals. The meal was accompanied by an invitation to the deceased to rise and join the living in food and drink. These meals were offered to keep the memory of the dead alive, to give the deceased food to sustain them in the afterlife, and as a means of protection from intrusion by spirits of the dead. In both the East and West, a libation was poured, followed by a meal. Roman frescoes portray women as the hosts of these banquets and raising a cup to toast the deceased. In the East, grave steles suggest that women also had a leading role at funerary banquets. They depict the deceased male householder reclining and his wife sitting before a three-legged table, on which food and wine are placed (see Figure 5.3). In the East, wine was sometimes poured through a pipe or into a vase that emptied on the deceased (the idea being that it sustained the shadowy departed in Hades), and a garland of flowers was placed over the tomb. In Rome the meal took place in a variety of locations. The wealthy celebrated funerary banquets in family mausoleums or columbaria, reclining on *klinai*; others gathered outside the grave and sat on the ground on cushions arranged in a semicircle, a custom that was also practiced in the East; still others possibly gathered in catacomb chambers furnished with benches carved out of the tufa (volcanic rock) and decorated with scenes of banqueting, although the stench of the dead and poor lighting of these spaces have led some scholars to reject this idea.

FICTIVE KINSHIP

Finally, we turn to the uses of what anthropologists call "fictive kinship language," a phrase that describes the uses of familial language to represent the relationships of people not bound by blood or traditional family ties. Fictive language appears in the New Testament, where it describes God as father, mother, or lord, and where writers describe themselves and their audiences as fathers, children, brothers, sisters, slaves, and freedpersons. Paul is fond of representing himself and his coworkers as *oikonomoi*, a term usually translated as "steward" in modern translations (1 Cor. 4:1, 9:17; Eph. 3:2; Col. 1:25; also Titus 1.7). A closer rendering might be "chamberlain," as an *oikonomos* was typically a slave that a *kyrios* entrusted with the most important responsibilities of his household. The Johannine Epistles describe believers as children (1 John 2:14, 18; 3:1, 10; 5:2, 19; 2 John 1, 4, 13; 3 John 4) or even "little children" (1 John 2:1, 12, 28; 3:7, 18). 2 John 1 represents Christians as the children of "an elect lady [*kyria*]," a description that portrays believers as belonging to the household of an elite woman who faithfully conducts her household duties on behalf of her *kyrios*. This usage parallels to some degree what one finds in the Greco-Roman world, where, for example, benefactors of cities were given the honorary title "father of the city," and members of trade associations sometimes called patrons mothers or fathers and each other brothers and sisters, as did devotees of particular religions, who regularly styled themselves as slaves of their god or goddess. When people in the ancient world used such language to represent religious and communal identity and ideals, they imagined the kinds of relationships discussed above.

Fictive kinship language also appears in surprising ways. Paul, for example, represents himself as a wet nurse to Thessalonian believers (1 Thess. 2:7), a breastfeeding mother to Corinthians not yet ready for solid food (1 Cor. 3:1–3a), and a woman going back into labor on account of disobedience among Galatian believers (Gal. 4:19). Here, in contrast to Paul's invocation of an *oikodespotēs* disciplining wayward children in 1 Corinthians (4:14, 15, 21), the apostle invokes the traditional relationship of Greek mother with a child, an image that connoted tenderness and care.

It is possible that fictive kinship language created tensions in Christian assemblies. Paul asserts that in Christ there is no longer "slave or free" (Gal. 3:28), and in Philemon 16 he tells the master Philemon that he has sent Onesimus back to him "no longer as a slave but more than a slave, a beloved brother."

We may ask how a social network governed by laws of property and cultural values of patronage and clientship were practiced amid a new set of fictive kinship relations. The way fictive kinship language was used and understood probably depended on social and ritual context. In any case, tensions arising from usage could remain temporarily unresolved so long as Christians believed in an imminent return of Jesus, when the entire social order would be swept away. From a practical point of view, the New Testament development of household rules represents a more this-worldly solution for resolving inherent tension, namely through reciprocal responsibilities that recognized the status of each station and the obligations of respect and care that went along with them. Here, it is not a forthcoming eschatological revolution but the daily practice of service and mutual respect that serves to maintains hierarchical patterns, even while appealing to fictive kinship for their transformation.

THE SELF AND OTHERS

Those conflicts and disputes among you, where do they come from? Do they not come from your cravings that are at war within you?

—James 4:1

PEOPLE IN THE ROMAN WORLD did not understand themselves in the same way people do today. Perhaps one of the most important differences between ancient and modern notions of the self is that modern Western people celebrate individuality. The popular view is that one is free to do anything so long as it does not harm others. Education trains people not to follow the herd but to think independently. Ancients who thought about ethics would not have agreed with these notions and would have judged the individuality we champion today as an aberration. Their most celebrated people were not—as they are today—artistic outliers and geniuses, but rather those who best conformed to a set of virtues to which all were to aspire. For Aristotle, it is the mean that is golden, not the extreme. The mean here is not the average but the rightly balanced and tempered. It was Aristotle's widely shared view that only men could achieve this ideal, because only they had the reason and self-regulation to realize it. From a modern perspective, this idea is foreign and even exotic. It shows that the ancient world presents us with understandings of the self that are very different from our own.

Before the advent of Christianity, there were centuries of philosophical speculation concerning what constituted a self and the ways a person should regulate it. The maxim "Know yourself," was inscribed on the forecourt of the ancient temple of Apollo at Delphi. By the time of Plato, who referred to the inscription repeatedly, it was already ancient wisdom.[1] In succeeding centuries, philosophers wedded it to another maxim, "Care for yourself." What they meant was that those (usually male aristocrats) who wanted to rule their households and govern city-states properly needed to master themselves first. Again, we should not import modern understandings into these prescriptions. For example, ancient philosophers put great emphasis on self-knowledge derived from one's relation to others—what one classicist calls the "objective-participant" notion of the self—whereas moderns emphasize personal agency and reflection, the "subjective-individualist" model.[2] In other words, if modern people cherish personal agency and individual decision-making in conducting their lives, ancients conceived of themselves with reference to their location in communities and embedded relationships and interpreted themselves in the light of them.

Ancient authors had a fondness for lists of virtues and vices intended to shape selves for the common good of the polis and the household and to identify the vices of enemies of the social order. Such lists also occur in the New Testament, where they too have a social focus. An obvious parallel is found in Galatians 5:16–26, where Paul lists the virtues of the Spirit that draw believers together and the vices of the flesh that push them apart, concluding with a demand: "Let us have no self-conceit, no provoking of one another, no envy of one another" (v. 26). Paul and others intended such virtue and vice lists as communal portraits. Christians, in other words, are *this* kind of harmonious people; others are *that* kind of antisocial people.

This emphasis on virtues and vices did not promote pure group-think, however. Such language does not suggest that people were stereotypes, but rather that, when one thought of one's self, one also conceived of a set of socially shared goods. On an individual level, the presence of another in coming to know oneself was also crucial. Aristotle, for example, argued that we can only know virtue and vice by the ways they are reflected back to us through a friend. By recognizing greed or charity in a friend, I learn what it looks like within myself, the kind of character that produces virtue and vice, and what kind of behaviors to avoid.[3] Here the Other is a kind of mirror for the self. In the New Testament we find a version of this concept in Paul: "For now we see in a mirror, dimly, but then we will see face to face" (1 Cor. 13:12). Mirrors were expensive and rare objects in the ancient world, usually made of polished metal, and their reflective qualities offered only a blurred image of the self. Paul here is arguing that in the resurrection life to come, Christians will see themselves clearly as part of a creation completely freed from the powers of sin and death. Then, he argues, believers will discover the fullness of themselves as those made in Christ to love God and one another.

This object-participant model alerts us to the importance ancients placed on the Other in knowing oneself. It also resulted in a different way—literally—of seeing the world. Ancient optic theorization, for example, is, from a modern perspective, exotic, but it is helpful for recognizing some possible dimensions of some New Testament texts that a modern mindset might otherwise pass over. Ancient philosophers theorized that vision came about through physical rays reaching the eyes to create an image within the viewer—those rays either having been emitted by the object being viewed, or having been projected from the eyes and reflected back to them. The emission model helps to explain the reason that many were especially threatened by the "evil eye," a danger that continues to be feared in many Mediterranean cultures. Here, a malevolent stare from an enemy has the physical power to harm because of hostile rays emitted from the viewer that penetrate into an otherwise unprotected or unsuspecting self (think Godzilla's laser eyes). In antiquity, people wore amulets and placed images on their walls and outside their doors to ward off the evil eye. These notions of vision reflect what has been called the specular culture of antiquity, where appearance and honor, as well as shame and dishonor, were powerful tools of social control and self-identity. The fear of the evil eye represents the internalization of a larger social dynamic. The power of penetrating vision has left its trace in the Bible. The power of divine omni-surveillance is indicated in the Book of Revelation. In Revelation 2:18 the "Son of God" has "eyes like a flame of fire," and in Revelation 5:6 John sees a "Lamb standing . . . having seven horns and seven eyes, which are the seven spirits of God sent out into all the earth." The perfect power (seven horns) of a perfect gaze (seven eyes) follows an earlier set of messages to seven different churches in which, in each case, there is a description of what Jesus, the Lamb, knows (Rev. 2:2, 3, 9, 13, 19; Rev. 3:1, 8, 15). The church at Laodicea is threatened with the fear of exposure of nakedness as a form of divine public shaming (3:18). Seeing and knowing here are not mere observations; they represent a penetrating gaze.

What constitutes the self, where it is located, how one comes to know it, and what influences shape it are topics of centuries of philosophical reflection and argument. Philosophers continue to debate these topics today. New Testament scholars have come to differing conclusions about how biblical notions of the self and ethics intersected with larger philosophical systems and how their particular religious convictions rebounded to transform the cultural traditions that formed them. It is important to remember that biblical authors were not philosophers, nor did they have a detailed knowledge of ancient ethical systems of thought. It is unlikely that Paul and John the Revelator read treatises on optics. Still, as we will see, there is every reason to suppose that many biblical authors had a kind of popular eclectic knowledge of ethical theories and medical models of the self, as well as notions of training for virtue and the metaphysical schemes in which they were located. Such knowledge came with being a literate person living in the urban Greek world. Others, like the author of the Epistle of James, reflect an awareness of theorization of the self more at home in Jewish contexts, again in a more derived form. The cosmopolitan world in which Christianity developed furnished a series of concepts and ways of understanding that believers incorporated into their own religious frameworks and, one may argue, established the foundation for a new articulation of the self that continues to shape us today.

SOURCES OF THE SELF

In his study of the modern concept of the self, the philosopher Charles Taylor coined the phrase "sources of the self" to describe the constellations of factors that contributed to the emergence of the individual in modernity (an intellectual milieu having its philosophical beginning in sixteenth- and seventeenth-century Europe, and especially in the philosophy of Rene Descartes [1596–1650]). Among such factors Taylor includes social practices, ethical theories, aesthetic values, conceptualization of the physical world, medical knowledge, religious beliefs and rituals, and political understandings.[4] His notion of sources of the self proves useful for a discussion of notions and practices of self in antiquity. We have referred to the importance of knowing oneself through one's relations with another. Such an emphasis is symptomatic of the importance of honor and shame as social commodities foundational to antiquity's social order. There were also many other sources of ancient selves, including things like household duties, religious rituals, rites of passage, meals, prayers, civic festivals, entertainment, exercise, medical treatment, punishment, and the organization of private and public space—to name only a few. As Christianity developed and spread, engagement with traditions drawn from Judaism, as well as larger philosophical currents, brought about new and expanded ways of seeing the self.

Taylor's study of the emergence of the modern self reminds us that when we enter into the ancient world of the self we are stepping into a foreign cultural arena. Modernity introduced a set of distinctions that went on to shape the way many conceive the world around them. For our purposes we may describe this as a dualistic system that separates that which is scientifically observable and quantifiable from that which is not. Descartes distinguished two realms, the physical and the nonphysical, one belonging to the measurable physical order of creation, and the other belonging to an empirically unquantifiable domain of reason and theology. Corresponding to these two spheres, he distinguished between body and mind, creation and God, nature and the supernatural. For Descartes, the physical realm is a self-contained, material, and mechanistic system that is designed to run on its own and can be known through scientific observation and investigation; the nonphysical is a sphere outside of science that can only be known by logic and divine revelation. Ancient thinkers did not make these kinds of distinctions. While they conceived the world with sometimes dualistic categories, they were not those of Descartes or modernity. Rather than seeing the physical or natural world and the spiritual and supernatural world as separate spheres of existence, they tended to see them as belonging to one order, each defined by its respective place in a hierarchy of being and value. In the Cartesian view, there is a strict body-soul dualism; in ancient understandings, physical bodies and souls are not so separable.

Philosophers saw the self as a hierarchically organized compound of faculties wherein the true self or soul is located in powers of reason and deliberation, but is mixed together and affected by other powers of sensation, reproduction, appetite, and so on. The leading philosophical schools of the ancient world (broadly associated with Plato, Aristotle, Stoic philosophers, and Epicurus, whose ideas about the self we will consider later) conceived of this self and its constituent parts differently, but all placed priority on the role of reason and deliberation in the governance of the individual. As we will see, this priority proves to be important when we consider the ancient Greek notion of the spirit and compare it with Paul's understanding of the role of the Spirit in governing the body of Christ and the individual. Here it is sufficient to observe that in the ancient view, there is no such thing as modernity's divide between the natural and the supernatural; what we today call the supernatural, for ancients belonged to one end of a spectrum rather than a separate order. While the different points on the spectrum were in principle separable (Plato, for example, taught that one's eternal soul departs the body after death), they were nevertheless affected by one another.

Charles Taylor uses the phrase "the buffered self" to portray the modern self and "the porous self" to describe the more hierarchical understanding of premodernity.[5] In the latter case, the self is semipermeable; that is, it is less like a shell (buffered self) containing mechanisms of self-determination than it is the intersection of physical and metaphysical forces and a gradient of material and immaterial substances. Taylor traces the emergence of the buffered self to the Protestant Reformation, followed by the triumph of the scientific method and rationalism as the only valid means of knowing the world. The porous self, by contrast, he locates in an earlier sacramental understanding of reality, where the physical world is a means by which to know another domain interpenetrated by metaphysical realities. We see notions of a porous self in ancient beliefs about possession by good or evil spiritual forces, the ability to cast or suffer from spells and curses, and, as we will see below, in medical models of the body. Although few today champion Cartesian philosophy, Taylor contends that its dualistic framework remains an essential part of the mental equipment that we in the industrialized West continue to bring to the tasks of interpreting the world and conceiving of the self. Even if modern physics, physiology, and psychology challenge modernity's model of the buffered self, it remains an integral part of the "common sense" view of the world.

BODIES AND SELVES

The difference between the buffered dualist and the porous hierarchical self can be seen when we compare modern medical conceptions of the body with ancient ones. Modern medicine understands the body as a set of self-contained mechanical, physical, and biochemical functions that work together to maintain a biological homeostasis. The body can be broken down into organs, tissues, and cells, which in turn can be broken down into further subunits, which can be quantified by scientific measurement and understood according to physical laws. Greeks and Romans understood the body in a different way, and while their theories varied in details, they shared the basic framework of a hierarchical worldview that governed social relations generally. Hippocrates (460–370 BCE) furnishes us with the oldest surviving systematic framework of Greek medicine. His model was developed and expanded by a number of later figures, most notably Galen (130–216 CE). While not everyone followed their teachings, they are instructive for our discussion, as they all understood the body and its diseases according to a similar physiological system. The Hippocratic system is complex, but in general it theorized the body as composed of four primary elements—fire, air, water, earth—each with a corresponding secondary quality of hot, cold, wet, and dry. Each element, he argued, possesses a characteristic property and tendency. Fire and air are hot because air moves upward, and fire has a dynamic quality that refines, distills, and transforms. Water and earth are cold because water is heavy and flows or sinks downward, and earth is passive and receptive, reflecting its tendency to solidify or coagulate. Air and water are wet because, like fluids, they take the shape of their container and fill space. Fire and earth are dry because they refine and separate things. Hippocrates and Galen assigned each of the elements to a different part of the body. Finally, they associated each element with its own humor (which could be detected through educated scrutiny of bodily fluids), and each humor with a corresponding temperament having its own set of natural tendencies and personality traits. In this system, every human being is a unique combination of all four, exhibited through specific physical traits such as physique, the shape of the face, skin, appetite, metabolism, hair and eye color, color of urine, blood, stool, dreams, thought patterns, and personality. Proper diagnosis depends on close attention to physiognomy—scrutiny of a person through examination of his or her face—to determine what particular combination of humors the patient was born with.

On this model sickness results from *dyscrasia*, an imbalance of humors that arises through various means, one of the most important being ethical choices that run counter to the nature with which one was created. This could come about through excess eating, drinking, and so on, and also through other things such as too much or too little sex, exposure to too much or too little heat or cold, or dryness or wetness. Galen theorized that the cause of disease is the transgression of an unruly humor outside the boundaries of its allotted territory into another's, where it consumes the nutrients sustaining an adjacent humor. Death results when an unchecked humor takes over the entire body and destroys the body's balance. Maintaining or restoring the right balance (*eucrasia*) of the humors sustains health. For the Hippocratics, diagnosis and treatment included learning a patient's case history in order to determine what had been done to throw innate physical balance out of harmony. Galen specified that preserving health depended on the moderation of six things: air, food and drink, sleep and waking, motion (exercise) and rest, excretions and retentions, and passions of the mind. Immoderation in any of these disrupted the natural constitution of the body and manifested itself in pathology. Restoring *eucrasia* might include things such as changing a patient's environmental conditions to expose him or her to more heat or cold, or more dryness or moisture. Or a doctor might prescribe specific exercises and diet. Hippocrates and Galen were famous for the practices of venesection and bloodletting as a means of achieving *eucrasia*. It was also realized through other means, such as vigorous massage and cold baths.

Whereas modern people celebrate individuality and distinctiveness, this ancient medical model stresses the ideal of living in conformity with nature. This understanding had an influence that went far beyond the practice of medicine. We can detect its presence in the writing of the second-century Christian author and teacher Clement of Alexandria. In a treatise called the *Paedagogus* (Teacher), he devotes a good deal of attention to observations concerning things such as the way people walk, eat, sleep, dress, laugh, and have sexual intercourse.[6] He shares the Hippocratic view that such behaviors reveal and affect a person's bodily and spiritual health. For Clement, Christ works in a Christian's life as both doctor and teacher in order to bring about wellness. His workspace, however, is not the doctor's office or the classroom, but the church where believers assemble for worship and instruction. Similar to the Hippocratic physician, the divine Paedagogus seeks to bring about his patient's conformity to nature. For Clement this means using spiritual devotion and developing self-control to conform oneself as much as possible to the one true human nature, the image and likeness of God in which humankind was created (Gen. 1:26–27).

The Hippocratic system, exotic to most of us, was taken as common sense in the ancient world, and it invites us to reconsider traditional interpretations of some biblical texts. The dispute in Corinth over the Lord's Supper (1 Cor. 11:17–32) is a good example. In the Corinthian correspondence, Paul repeatedly refers to the church as the body of Christ (1 Cor. 10:17; 12:12, 18, 24, 27). We are inclined to think of this in metaphorical terms, but Paul has a much more physical understanding. In 1 Corinthians 12:4–27 he represents the assembly of believers as Christ's body animated by the divine Spirit. We are not very far from the ancient idea that the soul is a ruling faculty governing the body. Paul, however, conceives of this active power as Christ, or even the mind of Christ, controlling the whole. As in the case of human bodies, the church body must follow its governing power or it will suffer sickness. This idea is what Paul argues in 1 Corinthians 11 in a way that is, from a modern perspective, unexpected. Paul addresses problems that have erupted in Corinth over improper eating practices associated with immoderation at the Christ meal, which probably took place in the context of a banquet: some consume more food than others, so that a few are filled while others go hungry (v. 21). At public festivals as well as at more private meals at associations, ancient people were accustomed to the consumption of differing portions of food and wine depending on their social status. It is possible that Corinthian Christians have quantified the amount of food distributed to each member based on his or her social standing (a slave owner might get more than a slave, and a leader or patron more than the rest). Paul makes a strange observation, however, when he states that some Corinthians have become ill and died because they have failed to discern the body properly (v. 30). He goes on to suggest that this sickness and death is the result of bringing judgment on oneself. He casts the problem as arising from divisions (*schismata*) and factions (*haireseis*) in the body of Christ (vv. 18–19), two technical terms that have as their opposites the communal harmony and concord of the body politic. In later centuries the apostle's exhortation to discern the body of Christ rightly would turn into a debate concerning how bread and wine should be understood sacramentally as the body and blood of Christ (as transubstantiation, real presence, spiritual presence, or memorial). However, it is notable that Paul links sickness and death with a communal body of Christ divided against itself, and that he prescribes self-examination (v. 28) as a necessary means of avoiding divine judgment. This statement is not to suggest that a medical model furnishes a sole explanation for Paul's remarks concerning death and sickness (v. 27, for example, attributes them to consumption in an unworthy fashion). Nevertheless, for listeners who had already been shaped through popular conceptions of medicine to conceive of sickness and health by reference to physical imbalance and internal discord of humors, the link between sickness, death, and overeating and drinking would have been immediately comprehensible.

GENDER AND THE SEX THAT IS ONE

The four elements constituting the body were theorized according to a hierarchical gradient of being and dynamics, ranging from fire, the lightest and most active element, to earth, the heaviest and most passive one. Here biological theory concerning the determination of the gender of a human embryo is telling and shows how an understanding of the human body as hierarchically arranged is at home in the ancient world's view of hierarchical relations more broadly. Unlike modern medicine, which understands an embryo's physical traits and determination of sex genetically, ancients looked to factors accompanying gestation. According to Hippocrates, what determines an embryo's sex is the degree of heat and dryness in the womb. If there is insufficient heat and too much moisture, embryos develop into girls. Cold, wet wombs produce weak and female infants and lesser males. Hot, dry ones result in robust males. Following the same theory, Aristotle asserted that women are incomplete males, since they do not receive the necessary heat and dryness in the womb to become male. Maleness and femaleness exist on a spectrum determined by the amount of heat, dryness, cold, moisture, and hardness or softness. Men who gestate in a too moist and cool womb emerge as soft or effeminate. Galen prescribed cold baths for such males in order for them to realize their proper balance of hot/cold, dry/moist, and hard/soft. It is worth noting that, unlike modern conceptions that often link effeminacy with homosexuality, there was no such association in the ancient world. The main concern was not with same-sex relations, but rather with self-control and male power over others. Excess was associated with softness and feminization. Clement of Alexandria associated foppery with feminizing self-indulgence in oils, creams, food, sex, and soft clothing. This is the opposite of the believer properly masculinized by the regulation of Christ. John the Baptist, clothed in camel's hair and feeding on locusts, was a man's man.[7]

All these ideas suggest that while one may have been born male, conception, gestation, and birth were only the first stages toward becoming masculine. Exercise, for example, continued the process of becoming a man and preserved masculinity. When Paul used athletic language to describe his faith, listeners would have heard an affirmation of his manliness: "Athletes exercise self-control in all things; they do it to receive a perishable wreath, but we an imperishable one. So I do not run aimlessly, nor do I box as though beating the air; but I punish my body and enslave it" (1 Cor. 9:25–27). He also invited Christians to imagine him as a manly apostle when he furnished them with a catalogue of the trials he had endured for the Gospel (1 Cor. 4:11; 2 Cor. 11:23–29; also 1 Tim. 4:7–8; 1 Pet. 1:13). Endurance was the hallmark of masculinity in the ancient world. The second-century satirist Lucian, for example, celebrated the philosopher Demonax (c. 70–170 CE) for cultivating physical fitness: "He . . . trained his body and cultivated toughness."[8] He goes on to describe how Demonax cared for himself by seeking to live according to the masculine ideal of self-sufficiency or self-government. Again, the parallel with Paul is striking, as he often makes a point of not seeking the support of anyone (1 Thess. 2:9; 2 Thess. 3:8). In the verses leading to Paul's stylization of himself as an athlete, he makes the point that he supported himself when he was at work among the Corinthians (1 Cor. 9:1–23). Paul couches his athletic training and self-sufficiency in the portrait of his dedication to the Gospel, but in the cultural code of his day, it also demonstrates Paul's manliness as well as his virtue.

These accounts of physiological development and gender were at home in a world where a hierarchical political and economic order was seen as natural. The theories of Hippocrates, Aristotle, Galen, and others were developed in societies governed by male elites and organized for their benefit. On this understanding, the hot/cold, dry/moist, hard/soft dichotomization of sex and gender expresses a hierarchy of power wherein the male/strong/active/dominant rules the female/weak/passive/subservient, and, as a consequence of their natural constitutions, different personality types are better suited for governance than others. Males and females are born, but men and women are made through regimes of (self) mastery. Thus, in his treatise *On Household Management*, Xenophon has Socrates describe the way the householder Ischomachus had to learn first to master himself before he could marry and turn to mastering his young wife.[9] Thus, the active/passive motif runs through the self even as it does through the household. Further, a higher natural mix of the active/male results in the governance of the higher proportion over the passive/female. Clement of Alexandria echoes Xenophon's orientation when he describes the relative capacity of men and women to regulate themselves. Improperly trained wives, he argues, like to dress seductively and wear fancy jewelry, and worse than such women are men who feminize themselves through the pursuit of luxury: "For if the female sex, on account of their weakness, desire more, we ought to blame the habit of that evil training, by which often men reared up in bad habits become more effeminate than women."[10]

These notions about gender can be found in the New Testament. They furnish a biologically laden understanding of the claim of 1 Peter 3:7 that women are "the weaker sex" and the Pastor's exhortation that "women should dress themselves modestly and decently in suitable clothing, not with their hair braided, or with gold, pearls, or expensive clothes, but with good works, as is proper for women who profess reverence for God" (1 Tim. 2:9–10; see also, 1 Pet. 3:3–4). The next verse instructs them to "learn in silence with all submissiveness" (v. 11). Ischomachus tells Socrates that the first thing he had to do after he married his fourteen-year-old wife was to teach her to keep quiet, and then to instruct her that it is virtue—not makeup and jewelry — that makes a woman.[11] Without him, the argument supposes, she would remain untamed—chatty, made-up, and luxuriously adorned. In the Pastorals, *young* widows (i.e. both unmarried and formerly married single women) who do not (re)marry "grow wanton . . . they learn to be idlers, gadding about from house to house, and not only idlers but gossips and busybodies, saying what they should not" (1 Tim. 5:11–13). The Pastor's advice: "I would have younger widows marry, bear children, rule their households and give the enemy no occasion to revile us" (v. 14). The ancient medical teachings of the Hippocratic tradition (which the text does not invoke but is certainly at home within) would certainly have agreed: women are, with reference to gestation, half-baked men, but they can still aspire to being more masculine and realize what nature makes possible for them, with the help of more naturally self-possessed men. "Upon my word," Socrates exclaims upon learning how well Ischomachus has formed his wife to be, "your wife has a truly masculine mind!"[12] Given the masculinist discourses that shaped Paul and his audiences' common-sense view of the world, Paul's gender-bending descriptions of himself as a wet nurse (1 Thess. 2:7), even a woman in labor (Gal. 4:19), as well as the erasure of gender distinctions in Galatians 3:25–28, are especially remarkable.

However objectionable these ideas may seem from a modern Western perspective, the kinds of gender associations we see in 1 Peter and 1 Timothy prevailed across a vast spectrum of relations and social organizations in the Roman world. Ancients saw them displayed all around them, not just in the way their daily lives and practices were organized, but also iconographically in the depiction of ruling elites in statues, on reliefs, and even on the coins they used in everyday transactions. Portraiture used balance and symmetry as well as the representation of sober facial expressions to celebrate their aristocratic male subjects as self-possessed and governed by virtue; noble women were similarly portrayed with hair elaborately coifed and clothing properly arranged, designating their domestic regulation and matronly virtues. An instructive example of both gender regulation and mastery can be seen in a relief from a first-century temple dedicated to the worship of Augustus and his Julio-Claudian successors at Aphrodisias. It belongs to a series of depictions of emperors as victors over their enemies and as figures numbered among the Olympian gods. In one of them (Figure 6.1), the male/female, active/passive, dominant/subject

FIGURE 6.1 Sebasteion relief, Aphrodisias, first century CE. Photo by author. Aphrodisias Museum, Aphrodisias, Turkey.

gender code is displayed through a depiction of the standing, stoic-looking Emperor Claudius, depicted as a heroic male nude. A trophy (the armor of a defeated enemy) in his right hand signifies his military victory and prowess. Both the nudity and the trophy convey the emperor's masculinity and power, as well as his natural and divinely given right to rule others. A stricken female figure personifying the vanquished enemy kneels below the trophy. Her posture represents her subjugation, while her unbound hair, the dress that slips off her shoulder to reveal a bare breast and her display of emotion symbolize both her grief and lack of regulation. This is a highly coded relief. It feminizes the enemy and, in the gender code we have been discussing, renders it as passive, weak, wild, and deserving of masculine mastery. By contrast, the sober figure to Claudius's left, personifying the Roman Senate, is a properly coifed and dressed, regulated, and temperate matron.

These contrasts reveal the social currency of the naturalized gender codes we have been discussing. It is not surprising to discover Christians invoking them by teaching that husbands are the heads of women (1 Cor. 11:3; Eph. 5:23) exhorting women to be submissive to men (Eph. 5:22; Col. 3:18; 1 Pet. 3:1), or, based on the order of creation, forbidding women from having any authority over men (1 Tim. 2:11–14). These examples are not to suggest that we should read the New Testament through the lens of what we see at Aphrodisias or in ancient medical textbooks. Paul and his followers do not base their promotion of the headship of men over women on the basis of biological theories of gender formation, but rather on the derivation of Eve from Adam, and on her seduction of him (1 Cor. 11:8–9; 1 Tim. 2:13–14). The passages rather reveal how common a hierarchical theory of gender was in the ancient world.

SELF-MASTERY AND VIRTUE

There is no single model of the self in the New Testament, nor even, it appears, within the literature directly from Paul. In 1 Thessalonians 5:23 the apostle, for example, writes (in passing) of a self made of three parts: body (*sōma*), soul (*psychē*) and spirit (*pneuma*). Elsewhere he refers to spirit and flesh (*sarx*; see, for example, 1 Cor. 5:5; 2 Cor. 7:1), spirit and body (1 Cor. 7:34), mind (*nous*) and body or flesh (Rom. 7:22–25; see Eph.

2:3; Col. 2:13), and spirit and mind (1 Cor. 14:14–19). When he refers to *pneuma*, it is not always clear whether one should translate it with an uppercase "P" (with reference to the divine Spirit) or a lowercase "p," with respect to a mortal one (Rom. 8:15). Scholars debate whether Paul had a consistent view, one that developed over time, or an ad hoc understanding applied to the situation he was addressing. Many argue that he reflects a religious and philosophical eclecticism characteristic of the New Testament period, when four main philosophical schools that had developed independently in earlier centuries were joined together into a popular eclecticism with which relatively literate people such as Paul would have been familiar. Here we introduce the four broad systems associated with Plato, Aristotle, the Stoics, and Epicurus. Each of them shared a hierarchical model of the self, distinguished the soul from the body, saw the soul as the center of intelligence, localized in or associated with a particular part of the body, and associated mental and moral faculties with the soul, not the body. All four championed self-mastery (*enkrateia*)—control of desires and passions—as a chief good. This term recurs with regularity across the New Testament (Acts 24:25; 1 Cor. 7:9, 9:25; Gal. 5:23; Titus 1:8; 2 Pet. 1:6). Plato and Aristotle, unlike the Stoics and Epicureans, believed that the soul had rational and irrational aspects, and that the soul continued to exist for a period after death, which was when the soul separated from the body.

Plato theorized that a person is a body and soul, with the soul consisting of three parts: the *logistikon* (reasoning), *thymoeides* (spirited), and *epithymētikon* (appetitive).[13] It is instructive that the terms *thymoeides* and *epithymētikon* both have as their root the Greek word for passion or longing (*thymos*). Plato likened the three faculties to three classes of a society, with the *logistikon* ruling the city-state, the *thymoeides* defending it, and the *epithymētikon* producing its material goods. The *logistikon* is the ruling faculty of the soul that governs the other two below it, through its capacity to reason and distinguish appearances from reality. The *thymoeides*, or high-spirited part of the soul, is the intermediate faculty by which we become angry or get into a temper. The *epithymētikon*—the opposite of the *logistikon*—is the lowest part of the soul, by which one experiences hunger, thirst, pleasure, and carnal erotic love. The *thymoeides*, as the middle part of the soul, can be aligned rightly with the *logistikon* to transform high spirit into indignation, courage, and a desire for justice; when improperly aligned with the *epithymētikon*, it seeks bodily pleasure and sensuality. A life governed by the *epithymētikon* misuses both the *logistikon* and *thymoeides* in a life driven by desire and pleasure. The cartoon character Homer Simpson is a good example of a person directed by the *epithymētikon*. The rightly regulated life, by contrast, expresses itself in what Plato named the four leading virtues: wisdom (*phronēsis*), courage (*andreia*), temperance (*sōphrosynē*), and justice (*dikaiosynē*).[14] Later (middle and neo-) Platonists coined the word *metriopatheia*, "the (correct) moderation of the passions," to describe the balancing of passion and reason in leading a life directed by virtue.

Aristotle's view of the self was based on a different hierarchical model of the soul. For him, different degrees of souls animate three different orders of living things (plants, animals, and humans). The soul, broadly speaking, is the form or essence of a thing that allows it to realize its full potential. Each higher soul possesses the one(s) below it and is distinguished by its operation. Thus, moving from lowest to highest, plants have nutritive souls manifested by nutrition, growth, and reproduction; animals have sensitive souls with the potential for sensation, locomotion, perception, and appetite, as well as the capacity to desire outcomes (such as a rabbit wanting to save its life by running away from a predator); humans have rational souls, realized by deliberation, judgment, knowledge, and rational thought. Aristotle considered the reasoning faculty of humans as the highest order of the soul, whose essence is to govern the soul's lesser powers. He theorized that the good or happy life is achieved when one governs oneself and tempers one's desires through reason, in accordance with the leading virtues listed above, in addition to a number of other ones: magnanimity, liberality, and gentleness.[15] The virtuous life is the outcome of learning to use reason and desire to do the right thing at the proper time in the correct measure. Here, Aristotle again engages in a gendered understanding of what such a life is like. Males, for example, are expected to achieve a full expression of wisdom, courage, temperance, and justice, whereas women are to do so to the degree that their natural limits permit and social location require. The same virtues apply to all, but the form of virtue differs according to one's gender. Thus, for example, the virtue of temperance (*sōphrosynē*) describes a state of total self-mastery for males, but of modesty and chastity for women. The Pastoral Epistles are not Aristotelian, but they nevertheless manifest a gendered notion of the virtues in the use of the word *sōphrosynē* to describe a virtue that both men and women are to follow, but to deploy in different ways. The NRSV rightly captures the nuances when it translates *sōphrosynē* as "temperate" or "self-controlled" when applied to men (1 Tim. 3:2; Titus 1:8; 2:2, 6) but as "modest in appearance" when applied to women (1 Tim. 2:9). For men it refers to being masters of themselves and their family members; for women it appears in a catalogue describing chastity and household duties (Titus 2:4). Aristotle argued that women, being incomplete males, find their full end in domesticity and under the governance of males.

While Aristotle celebrated self-control as a male ideal, he argued that many fail to achieve it because of being buffeted by desire. He (like Plato) linked the failure to master the self with *acrasia* (literally, "without governance"), a state that occurs when one knows the right thing to do but, because of desire or passions and weakness, fails to carry it out. Such a person is bound for unhappiness. Those who followed Aristotle, developing Plato's term *metriopatheia*, coined the word *metriopathēs* to describe this rightly measured use of reason and desire in ethical decision-making. It is interesting to compare this concept with Paul's representation of the disordered self in Romans 7:14–25, where he describes a situation in which someone knows and wants to do the good that God commands in one's "inmost self" (v. 22), but instead follows another power in one's "members" (v. 23). He goes on to describe such a self as being at war with itself. Unlike Aristotle, however, Paul does not believe that rightly learning to reason and behave in accordance with virtue is what leads to a solution to this quandary, since the problem for Paul arises from a kind of hostile takeover of creation by the power of sin, and hence requires repossession by God. *Metriopathēs* is not the way out of Paul's quandary. What is needed is a complete makeover of the person as a new creation. The New Testament is filled with language exhorting believers to train themselves to live in accordance with virtues. For Paul such training belongs to the crafting of a new self that comes about through participation in the life of the resurrected Jesus. In other words, Paul shares a discourse of ethical training with his contemporaries, but it is built into a new formulation that results in a transposition of a preexisting tradition to an eschatological framework located in an assembly of believers. The setting thus moves from the household and the polis to the community of Christians and their relations with one another in worship and common life. This movement into a new social and temporal formulation resulted in a profound transformation of a preexisting ethical tradition.

A third hierarchical model of the self is found among a body of philosophers called the Stoics. Stoicism derives its name from the Stoa, a colonnaded hall at the Athenian agora where its founder, Zeno (c. 334–262 BCE), taught. Unlike Plato, who argued that humans had a soul with three faculties with rational and irrational components, Stoics conceived the self holistically as an expression of the larger cosmos. They viewed the cosmos as a living being formed, penetrated, and held by the divine *pneuma*, which they conceived as a subtle material fire mixed into the entire universe that keeps it whole and in harmony according to an inherent *logos* (reason, rational order, logic). They also conceived this *logos* as mind (*nous*). The universe has an immanent rationality that people can know and conform themselves to follow. In distinction from Plato and Aristotle, who based their system on a dualist view of body and soul, the Stoics were monists—that is, they understood all things as a bodily unity and a manifestation of *pneuma*. Stoicism taught there is an eternal recurrence of the cosmos, with each cycle ending in conflagration or *ekpyrōsis*. The unending cycle of the universe is movement from *ekpyrōsis* to fire-formed material and back again, in a series of equally identical iterations. As Woody Allen once asked, musing on another picture of eternal recurrence (that of Friedrich Nietzsche), "Does this mean I will have to sit through the Ice Capades again?" The Stoics' answer would be, "Yes, exactly the way you have always done it. Mercifully, though, you won't remember the last time."

According to Stoicism, the self is a unified and rational consciousness, represented by a governing faculty, the *hēgemonikon*, which, when ruling correctly, expresses itself in virtue. Virtue is manifested in a life lived in accordance with nature, with the ordering *logos* of the cosmos, with the way things really are. Vice, on the other hand, reflects a misunderstanding of nature and manifests choices in conflict with reality. The Stoics also theorized the problem of *akrasia*, but, following their monist cosmology, instead of accounting for it as a war between faculties of corporeal desiring and transcendent reasoning, they conceived it as a cognitive problem of understanding, which to be set right needed a capacity for true perception. A central task of philosophical training was to learn to distinguish reality from illusion and truth from falsehood in order to conform oneself as much as possible to the *logos*. In opposition to the philosophical ideals of *metriopatheia* and *metriopathēs* (the rational soul's right use of desires) championed by Platonists and Aristotelians, the Stoics taught *apatheia*, freedom or detachment from desire, as the ethical goal. The ruling faculty of a self that is in conformity with nature is able to discern the world around it properly and make correct ethical choices in conformity with the *pneuma* that animates and keeps all things intact; it is not swept about by impulses that drive people to do irrational and self-harming things, all the while thinking that what they are doing is correct and good for them. *Oikeiōsis* is another important Stoic term that describes the knowledge of and accommodation to that which belongs to oneself. When one comprehends oneself and one's place in the cosmos rightly, one also understands one's obligations to others and adapts to them. The Stoics taught that it is not enough to follow rules of right behavior; one must also understand the principle that makes an ethical choice correct, rational, and in conformance with the ordering of the cosmos. That way, when faced with an ethical dilemma, a person will be directed not by arbitrary-seeming obligations but by profound principles consistent with nature. Mr. Spock of *Star Trek* presents us with a sci-fi version of the Stoic sage who lives a life of *apatheia* consistent with what is rational and what nature requires.

Some scholars detect the presence of Stoic cosmology in the New Testament. For example, in 2 Peter (3:7–8, 10–13), there is a possible appropriation of the Stoic notion of *ekpyrōsis* in the author's description of the Second Coming accompanied by a total sweeping away of all things in a fiery annihilation that dissolves and melts the elements. A number of other ideas are arguably influenced by Stoic teachings: the author's exhortation not to be carried away by people who lose their "stability"

(3:17); the assurance that, through divine power and promises, believers can "escape corruption that is in the world because of lust, and become participants of the divine nature" (1:4); and the way the author describes creation coming into being and ending in fiery conflagration "by the word [*logos*] of God" (3:5, 7). This is not to argue that the author is a Stoic, only that popular currents of Stoicism may have shaped his thinking.

Some also see Stoic connections in Paul's treatment of the church as the body of Christ in 1 Corinthians 12:12–31, and in his explanation of the resurrection body in 1 Corinthians 15:35–49. In 1 Corinthians 12:12–31 Paul emphasizes the interconnection and mutual dependence of the believers who form one body by the Spirit into whom they have been baptized (v. 12), so that each member has a particular place and function (vv. 14–25) and the different members are appointed to particular tasks (vv. 27–31). Some see the influence of the Stoic notion of *oikeiōsis* and the *pneuma* interpenetrating and holding creation together in this passage. In 1 Corinthians 15:35–49 the apostle, discussing the physical resurrection of the dead, distinguishes between a physical body and a spiritual body, each animated by a life-giving spirit (vv. 44–46). His case for the resurrection of the body includes reference to various forms of corporeality: one for humans, another for animals, another for birds, and another for fish (all of which he names as flesh). Another he distinguishes, like the Stoics, as celestial and terrestrial bodies, each ranked according to its own glory (sun, moon, and stars; 15:39–41). The way Paul weds the language of flesh and terrestrial/celestial bodies with the idea of a life-giving spirit (*pneuma*) echoes the Stoics, since for the philosophers it is a single animating *pneuma* that suffuses all things. All of this is, however, placed in a decidedly non-Stoic-sounding framework when he links the coming transformation of all things from physical to spiritual, with an apocalyptic notion of the second coming of Jesus (15:51–56).

Finally, there is the model of self and cosmos connected with Epicurus (341–270 BCE) and his followers. If the Stoics conceived all things as composed of *pneuma*, Epicurus, following the pre-Socratic philosopher Democritus (c. 460–c. 370 BCE), argued that everything is composed of tiny particles or atoms that occupy empty space. These continually detach themselves from objects around us and form images of themselves within us, giving us the means to perceive the world. For Epicureans, death marks the end of existence. In the meantime, nature teaches us to pursue pleasure and avoid pain, and that that which brings about the greatest pleasure is what wise people should pursue. Epicurus was not a hedonist, however; he did not promote the idea that one should do whatever gives immediate gratification, but rather that one should sacrifice trivial, immediate pleasures and embrace hardship in order to achieve significant and lasting pleasure. For example, a greater pleasure will derive from studying and passing an exam on the salient features of Epicureanism than from going out with friends to a party, failing the exam, and not graduating.

The task of the philosophical life is to know what pains to endure in order to maximize the happiest outcome. An extravagant lifestyle of self-indulgence leads ultimately to an unhappy outcome because it destroys one's capacity for perfect health. The one who rightly knows which pleasures to pursue and which pains to avoid, in the correct measure, achieves the goal of self-sufficiency (*autarkeia*) and enjoys a life of tranquility.

Epicurus's philosophy is paradoxical and easily caricatured. Paul does this when, invoking an Epicurean slogan, he contrasts hope for the resurrection life to come with a life dedicated to pleasure: "If the dead are not raised, 'Let us eat and drink, for tomorrow we die'" (1 Cor. 15:32). Some detect an Epicurean influence on Paul's exhortation to the Thessalonians to pursue a quiet life of contentment, free from care and anxiety, so that they may be "dependent on no one" (1 Thess. 4:9–12). However, the basic Epicurean idea that one should accept short-term pain to achieve long-term gain pervades the whole of the New Testament.

JEWS AND THE SELF

It is not possible to draw a hard and fast distinction between Hellenistic and Jewish understandings of the self. The first-century Jewish philosopher Philo of Alexandria, for example, used an eclectic tradition comprising Platonist, Aristotelian, and Stoic ideas to exegete the Hebrew Scriptures. He deployed notions of the self discussed above, but wedded them to biblical concepts to create new formulations. For example, from the stories of the patriarchs (Abraham, Isaac, Jacob, and Joseph) and heroes such as Moses, he drew illustrations of stages of the soul's upward progress—how the soul, through self-mastery of passions, could traverse the vast spiritual distance from a pit of sensuality to the very presence of God. Moses, who climbed Mount Sinai and saw God, represents the pinnacle of what God intends for humans. Philo interpreted Genesis 1–2 as the story of a two-stage human creation. The first stage, represented by Genesis 1:27, designates a spiritual and everlasting being created in the image of God, and therefore possessing *nous* and *logos*, humanity's reasoning capacities, which distinguish humans from the rest of creation. The second stage, found in the account of Genesis 2:4–8, where God makes Adam from the ground (*adamah*), represents the corporeal creation that enables humans to sense the world and learn about the divine from physical experience. Philo interprets Genesis 2:7 ("then the Lord God formed man from the dust of the ground, and breathed into his nostrils the breath of life") as the completion of creation. The image of God is the part of humans animated by the divine *pneuma*, wedded to corporeal existence. This idea of a two-stage creation sets the framework for a Platonic model of the self as ideally engaged in a steady growth of the spirit's self-mastery over the desires of the body, in a movement of ever more likeness to and purer contemplation of God and understanding of the world. He even allegorizes Adam as the life of the mind and Eve as that of the senses, thus replicating the gendered understanding of males and females discussed above. Here we can see how Philo weds biblical traditions with a Hellenistic philosophical heritage of the care and mastery of the self.

The wedding of Scripture with a hierarchical model of a higher faculty ruling over lower ones is a theme that runs through much of intertestamental literature roughly contemporary with the New Testament. *Fourth Maccabees* (first century CE) depicts the martyrdom of the Jewish priest Eleazar and the Maccabean brothers by the Syrian king Antiochus IV Epiphanes in 167 BCE, when the Hellenistic ruler persecuted those refusing to acknowledge his divinity and conform themselves to the Hellenization of Jerusalem and the Second Temple. The document celebrates its protagonists' faithfulness to the Law as the means of their control of passions that otherwise would have led them to apostasy. The author affirms the superiority of reason over passions and desires that he associates with the flesh, soul, and body, but believes that reason alone is not sufficient for self-mastery. One also needs to become wise—that is, educated in the Law and dedicated to right living (4 Macc. 1:15–17; 7:23). "*Devout* reason is governor of the emotions" (6:31; 7:16), the narrator affirms, thus uniting biblical tradition with Hellenistic models of self-mastery. The *Wisdom of Solomon* (second–first century BCE) similarly affirms a hierarchical model of the self as constituted by soul (*psychē, pneuma*) and body (*sōma*). Invoking a Stoic-sounding cosmology, it teaches that the immortal spirit of God—or, in Greek terms, divine *pneuma*—permeates all things (12:1), but it strikes out in a new direction when it claims that only with the special gift of God's holy spirit can humans become righteous and wise (7:7, 27; 9:4, 10, 17). Here wisdom (*sophia*) is a guide that resides in people and enables them to know all things and be righteous in their conduct.

Acrasia, the notion of a divided self at war with itself, as a natural consequence of higher faculties seeking to govern and tame lower ones (Plato and Aristotle), or of an incapacity to perceive the world properly (Stoicism), is a motif that runs through Greek and Roman reflection on the self and also appears in the New Testament. As we have seen, Paul offers a version of it in Romans 7:14–24. Another picture of *acrasia* appears in James 4:1–2, where the author sees the conflict of internal impulses as responsible for community discord: "Those conflicts and disputes among you, where do they come from? Do they not come from your cravings that are at war within you? You want something and do not have it; so you commit murder. And you covet something and cannot obtain it; so you engage in disputes and conflicts." Elsewhere, James refers to the divided self as "double-minded" (*dipsychos*, 1:8; 4:8). In 1:8 he refers to the double-minded as "unstable in every way," and in 4:8 the context links *dipsychos* with the passions at war within one's members. For James, double-mindedness arises by succumbing to one's own desire (*epithymia*, 1:14). An inclination to do evil because of desire is a theme that recurs in the Hebrew Bible and intertestamental literature. The Hebrew term for this inclination is *yēṣer*, a term that appears in Sirach (200–175 BCE) to describe an impulse in humans, misusing God's gift of free will, to sin (Sir. 15:11–20).

Both James and Sirach see God as the creator of *yēṣer/epithymia* (James 4:5; Sir. 15:14), and they call for the defeat of it through obedience to the Commandments. Here *epithymia* is not undifferentiated evil, but a consequence of desire not regulated to withstand temptation. In Sirach 21:11 it is those who observe the Law who gain mastery over their thoughts, a position James also adopts (2:8–26; 4:1–9). However, when unchecked, *epithymia* leads to a host of evils, many of which James describes (love of wealth—2:1–7; 5:1–6; lack of control of the tongue—3:6–12; divisions—4:1–11).

When we turn to more apocalyptic literature, the picture is very different. Documents from the Qumran community assert the existence of two spirits, one good and another evil, who exercise power and preside over the community of the righteous (i.e., those at Qumran) and the wicked (those outside it) (1QS 3:13–4.26). The Prince of Lights, the good spirit, governs the "sons of righteousness," and the Angel of Darkness rules over the "sons of perversity" (1QM 13:9–12). These powers and the communities they preside over will finally face off in a final apocalyptic battle when the Prince of Lights will conquer the Angel of Darkness. Additionally, there are two spirits, the Spirit of Truth and the Spirit of Perversity, that wage a war in the heart of each person until the end of the age and motivate people to do good and evil (1QS 4:2–11, 23–26). On this model, the self as battleground mirrors a larger cosmic war in which all of creation is involved.

With Paul, we come to another eschatological, arguably apocalyptic, model of the self. Here, once again, is the idea of an internal battle. Unlike what one finds in James and Sirach, Paul externalizes the source of the impulse to do evil. He sees the twin powers of Sin and Death at work in an enslaved creation pressing humans toward sin and disobedience of God's laws by stirring up passions that are associated with the flesh/body—its members "captive to the law of sin" (Rom. 7:5, 14, 22–23). For Paul, the two components of body/flesh and mind/spirit are supplemented by a third, the divine Spirit, who dwells in the believer to bring the self into right relationship with itself and with God. Paul can thus refer to his exterior body dying while his inner person awaits the resurrection and the full revelation of redemption (2 Cor. 4:7–12). He uses the language of victory and defeat, with the cross and resurrection as the means of God's conquest over Sin and Death, to celebrate a new identity where one no longer is enslaved by passions, subject to death and decay, but freed from them to be a child of God. For Paul, this release from bondage is coming not only to believers but to all of creation, which groans for its liberation (Rom. 8:19). The divine victory expresses itself in a new orientation of the self away from its warring passions and desires toward love of God and neighbor. It is won not by a personal conquest in a war within oneself—which Paul argues in Romans one is bound to lose—but rather by the victory of another, won on behalf of all creation—namely the conquest of death through the resurrection of Jesus. Thus, a new self is created, enabled to live the life of the spirit, no longer subject to Sin and Death, but subject to a new ruling power, the raised Jesus. For Paul, such a self is being animated even as the old self slips away en route to its appointed date with death. This new self, created after the image of Christ, expresses the new order that is present in the rule of the Spirit now—even while all of creation awaits its full arrival. Paul applies this concept more communally when he represents the assembly of believers as Christ's body, animated by the Spirit of God. For Paul, the assembly united spiritually to the resurrection of Christ is no longer under the power of Death and Sin. Full individuation of a believer comes by conforming oneself to the resurrection body that animates the church—by no longer following fleshly impulses, but instead being directed by the Spirit. He can even speak of having "the mind of Christ" (1 Cor. 2:16; Phil. 2:5), thus creating a kind of equation between the body of the church and the body of the believer, both of which are animated by the same power to realize their fullest selves both corporately and individually. One comes into one's fullness by conforming oneself to the new nature the resurrection of Christ has created.

We can see that by taking up themes from other philosophical and ethical traditions and integrating them with a new eschatology centered in Christ's death and resurrection, there is a transposition of philosophical concepts from a Greco-Roman to a Christian mental world. Incorporated into it, they offer both familiarity and enrichment through an understanding of the self as a battleground and the articulation of social ideals. For Paul, a hierarchical self meets and joins with a new identity invaded by God's spirit. This at once echoes and recasts a preexisting set of values and institutional orientations by reconfiguring them for ecclesial relations and formulations about creation. Paul's ideas would have sounded strangely familiar to his Greek and Roman contemporaries, but they would have been surprised to see how Paul used them to direct believers toward a new set of social goals and ideals. This new edifice of thought, created by Paul and the whole of the New Testament, is both the inheritance and the mental home of the secular West. Devout Christians today may strive to restore it, while secularists attempt to remodel it, and militant atheists seek to demolish it, but all have been formed within it. This inheritance shows that acquaintance with the imperial contexts of early Christ belief furnishes us not only with a better understanding of the Bible, but also of our own contexts and understandings of the self. Even as we find ourselves in a new set of secular understandings of the self, we discover that we have been formed by a long ethical tradition, refracted through biblical texts, modulated in new institutional arenas, and passed on in a variety of historical and cultural settings. The modern self one encounters when looking in a mirror represents innumerable selves made and remade by centuries of reflection.

NOTES

Chapter 1

1. The translation is from Michael W. Holmes, ed. and trans., *Apostolic Fathers: Greek Texts and English Translations*, 3rd ed. (Grand Rapids: Baker Academic, 2007).
2. Another volume in this series will take up the Gospels, writings that also reflect the sociocultural and political realities of the eastern Mediterranean, but in a way that deserves a dedicated discussion of its own.
3. For Mark and Peter, *Ecclesiastical History* 2.15.1–2; for Luke, 3.4.7 (based on Luke 1:2–3); for Matthew and John as eyewitness accounts of Jesus's ministry and their motives for writing their Gospels, 3.24.1–18. Eusebius states that John wrote his Gospel last to fill in gaps found in earlier accounts; later, in 6.14.5–7, he cites Clement of Alexandria (150–215) for the idea that he composed it to draw out the spiritual meaning of Jesus's life and teaching.
4. Justin, *Apology* 1.66, 67.
5. *Ecclesiastical History* 3.25.1–7; 3.3.5–7.
6. Michel de Certeau, *The Practice of Everyday Life*, translated by Steven Rendall (Berkeley: University of California Press, 1984).
7. See N. Tom Wright, *The Climax of the Covenant: Christ and Law in Pauline Theology* (Minneapolis: Fortress Press, 1993), 238.

Chapter 2

1. Hippolytus, *Apostolic Tradition* 16.4.
2. Tertullian, *On the Shows*.
3. Xenophon, *The Ephesian Tale of Anthia and Habrocomes* 1.2–3.
4. See *Pseudo-Marcellus, The Passion of the Holy Apostles Peter and Paul* and the Greek *Acts of Peter and Paul*, from the fifth or sixth centuries CE, in *The Ancient Martyrdom Accounts of Peter and Paul*, edited and translated by David L. Eastman (Atlanta: Society of Biblical Literature, 2015), 221–36.
5. Origen, *Against Celsus* 1.6, 71.

Chapter 3

1. For this data, Richard Duncan Jones, *Structure and Scale in the Roman Economy* (Cambridge: Cambridge University Press, 1990), 93–104.
2. Lucian, *The Passing of Peregrinus* 11–14.
3. Lucian, *Alexander the False Prophet* 18–19, 38–43, 55–58.
4. For the texts, see Margaret Williams, ed., *The Jews among the Greeks and Romans: A Diasporan Sourcebook* (Baltimore: John Hopkins University Press, 1998), 95–97, 109–11.
5. Pliny the Younger, *Letters* 10.96.
6. Origen, *Against Celsus* 2.30; 8.73.
7. Plutarch, *Precepts of Statecraft* 17.1 (*Moralia* 813E).
8. Suetonius, *Life of Vespasian* 23.4.
9. Frederick W. Danker, *Benefactor: Epigraphic Study of a Graeco-Roman and New Testament Semantic Field* (St. Louis, MO: Clayton, 1982), 217, slightly revised.

Chapter 4

1. Dio of Prusa, *Oration* 38.11, 43.
2. United Nations, "World Urbanization Prospects, the 2014 Revision [Highlights]," https://esa.un.org/unpd/wup/Publications/Files/WUP2014-Highlights.pdf.

3. United Nations, "World's Population Increasingly Urban with More Than Half Living in Urban Areas," July 10, 2014, http://www.un.org/en/development/desa/news/population/world-urbanization-prospects-2014.html.
4. From "Table 3: Built-Up Urban Areas by Urban Population Density," *Demographia World Urban Areas (Built-Up Urban Areas or Urban Agglomerations) 14th Annual Edition: April 2018* (http://www.demographia.com/db-worldua.pdf), 58–75. The urban areas (square kilometers) of these cities are: Dhaka, 368; Somalia, 91; Al-Raqqa, 31; London, 1,738; Chicago and environs, 6856.
5. Minucius Felix, *Octavius* 9.3–6.
6. Aelius Aristides, *Oration* 26.11, in *Aelius Aristides: The Complete Works*, 2 vols., edited and translated by Charles Allison Behr (Leiden: Brill, 1986).
7. Steven J. Friesen, "Poverty in Pauline Studies: Beyond the So-Called New Consensus," *Journal for the Study of the New Testament* 26 (2004): 323–61, at 339.
8. Emanuel Meyer, *The Ancient Middle Classes: Urban Life and Aesthetics in the Roman Empire 100 BCE–250 CE* (Cambridge, MA: Harvard University Press, 2012), 66.
9. *Shepherd of Hermas* 53.5 (*Parable* 4.5), in *Apostolic Fathers: Greek Texts and English Translations*, 3rd ed., edited and translated by Michael W. Holmes (Grand Rapids, MI: Baker Academic, 2007).
10. *Shepherd of Hermas* 50.1–2 (*Parable* 1.1–2; translation by Holmes).
11. Origen, *Against Celsus* 3.55, in *Origen: Contra Celsum*, edited and translated by Henry Chadwick (Cambridge: Cambridge University Press, 1980).
12. John Kloppenborg, "Gaius the Roman Guest," *New Testament Studies* 63 (2017): 534–49.
13. Josephus, *Antiquities of the Jews* 16.1162–65.

Chapter 5

1. *Acts of Paul and Thecla* 7–10.
2. A. Wallace-Hadrill, "*Domus* and *Insulae* in Rome: Families and Housefuls," in *Early Christian Families in Context: An*

Interdisciplinary Dialogue, edited by D. L. Balch and C. Osiek (Grand Rapids: William B. Eerdmans, 2003), 3–18.

3. Vitruvius, *On Architecture* 6.7.2, 5.
4. *Martyrdom of Justin* 2.
5. Richard Saller, "Corporal Punishment, Authority, and Obedience in the Roman Household," in *Marriage, Divorce and Children in Ancient Rome,* edited by Beryl Rawson (Oxford: Clarendon, 1991), 150.
6. Aristotle, *Politics* 1252^{a}1—1253^{b}20.
7. Xenophon, *On Household Management* 7.4—10.13.
8. Annette Huizenga, *Moral Education for Women in the Pastoral and Pythagorean Letters* (Leiden, the Netherlands: Brill, 2013), 59–76. Huizenga presents an annotated translation of the letters mentioned here, as well as the rest of the corpus.
9. Suzanne Dixon, "The Sentimental Ideal of the Roman Family," in *Marriage, Divorce and Children in Ancient Rome,* edited by Beryl Rawson (Oxford: Clarendon, 1996), 99–113.
10. Plutarch, *Advice to a Bride and Groom* (*Moralia* 142F, 145B–146A).
11. General Assembly Resolution 44/25, *Convention on the Rights of the Child,* A/RES/44/15 (20 November 1989). Available from un.org/documents/ga/res/44/a44r025/.
12. Philo, *Special Laws* 3.110; see also Pseudo-Phocylides, *Sentences* 11.184–85; Josephus, *Against Apion* 2.202; 1.60.
13. Pliny, *Panegyricus* 27.1.
14. *Panegyricus* 21.1–4, also 2.1, 29.2, and 67.1.
15. Plutarch, *The Education of Children* 12 (*Mor.* 9A).
16. *Against Apion* 2.204.
17. Petronius's (27—66 CE) *Satyricon* is an entertaining account of the excesses and social incompetence of a wealthy freedman named Trimalchio; it reflects the attitudes of a snobby elite looking down on a new class of social climbers.
18. See, for example, Wayne Meeks, *The First Urban Christians: The Social World of the Apostle Paul,* 2nd ed. (New Haven, CT: Yale University Press, 2003), 22–23.

Chapter 6

1. See, for example, Plato, *Protagoras* 343B, where ancient sages who circulated the maxim are listed; see also *Philebus* 48C, where he has Socrates state that those who know themselves will have more success understanding others.
2. Christopher Gill, *Personality in Greek Epic, Tragedy, and Philosopher: The Self in Dialogue* (Oxford: Oxford University Press, 1998).
3. See, for example, *Nicomachean Ethics* 1169b–1170b; *Eudamaean Ethics* 1244b–1245a; and *Magna moralia* 2.15.1213a.
4. Charles Taylor, *Sources of the Self: The Making of the Modern Identity* (Cambridge, MA: Harvard University Press, 1989).
5. Charles Taylor, *A Secular Age* (Cambridge, MA: Belknap Press, 2007), 35–41.
6. Clement of Alexandria, *Paedagogus*, Books 2–3.
7. Clement of Alexander, *Instructor* 2.11; *Miscellanies* 2.21–22.
8. Lucian, *Demonax* 4.
9. Xenophon, *On Household Management* 1.15–23; 7.4–15; 11.3–25.
10. Clement of Alexandria, *Instructor* 2.11.
11. *On Household Management* 7.10–14; 10.2–13.
12. *On Household Management* 10.1.
13. Plato, *Republic* 9.435e—445e; *Alcibiades* 130c.
14. First listed in *Republic*, Book IV, 427e; also *Protagoras* 330b.
15. Aristotle, *Rhetoric* 1366b1.

FURTHER READING

Chapter 1

Ehrman, Bart D., and Michael W. Holmes, eds. *The Text of the New Testament in Contemporary Research: Essays on the Status Quaestionis*. 2nd ed. Leiden and Boston: Brill, 2014.

Essays by leading experts discuss the manuscripts and sources for reconstructing critical editions of the Greek New Testament, as well as theological and social historical issues relating to text criticism.

Ferguson, Everett. *Backgrounds of Early Christianity*. Grand Rapids, MI: Eerdmans, 2009.

This is a thorough account of the social, political, philosophical, and religious contexts of the Roman, Jewish, and Greek world, and of the emergence of Christianity in the first two centuries.

Garnsey, Peter, and Richard P. Saller. *The Roman Empire: Economy, Society, and Culture*. 2nd ed. Berkeley: University of California Press, 2015.

This book offers a useful starting point for research into various aspects the Roman Empire (religion, economy, imperial administration, cities, households, and so on). Each chapter concludes with a summary of recent scholarship on the topic considered.

McDonald, Lee Martin, and James A. Sanders, eds. *The Canon Debate.* Peabody, MA: Hendrickson, 2008.
This volume is a collection of essays that take up detailed discussion by international scholars of the formation of both the Hebrew Bible and New Testament canon.

Chapter 2

Eidinow, Esther, and Julia Kindt. *The Oxford Handbook of Ancient Greek Religion.* Oxford: Oxford University Press, 2016.
This is a collection of introductory essays by leading scholars on a wide range of topics relating to ancient Greek religion, with engagement with previous scholarship and discussion of new methods of investigation.
Mikalson, Jon D. *Ancient Greek Religion.* 2nd ed. New York: John Wiley & Sons, 2011.
This is an illustrated introduction with a primary focus on the practices of ancient Greek religion; it includes a glossary and a list of resources for further study.
Price, S. R. F. *Religions of the Ancient Greeks.* Key Themes in Ancient History. Cambridge: Cambridge University Press, 1999.
An introduction to the ideas and practices of religion in different cities and periods of the Greek eastern Mediterranean, from the eighth century BCE through the fifth century CE, with a special focus on gender and cultural and political life.
Rüpke, Jörg. *From Jupiter to Christ: On the History of Religion in the Roman Imperial Period.* Translated by David M. B. Richardson. Cambridge: Cambridge University Press, 2014.
Rüpke's study focuses on the social practices and changing understanding of religion in the Mediterranean world of the first centuries CE.

Chapter 3

Ando, Clifford. *Imperial Ideology and Provincial Loyalty in the Roman Empire.* Berkeley: University of California Press, 2000.
Takes up the relationship of provinces to Roman power and the conduct of imperial policies, as well as the creation of political

consensus that allowed Rome to rule a vast territory with a limited bureaucracy for centuries.

Lintott, Andrew. *IMPERIUM ROMANUM: Politics and Administration*. London: Taylor & Francis, 2016.

This is a treatment of the various aspects of the Roman organization and administration of the empire, together with discussion of recent scholarship.

Price, S. R. F. *Rituals and Power: The Roman Imperial Cult in Asia Minor*. Cambridge: Cambridge University Press, 1986.

A classic study of the Roman imperial cult, its development and associated religious beliefs, and social and political function in Asia Minor, with close attention to material culture.

Zanker, Paul. 2002. *The Power of Images in the Age of Augustus*. 14th ed. Jerome Lectures 16. Translated by Albert Shapiro. Ann Arbor: University of Michigan Press, 2002.

With frequent use of images, this study explores the role and importance of imperial iconography in the establishment and promotion of Augustan rule.

Chapter 4

Harland, Philip A. *Associations, Synagogues, and Congregations: Claiming a Place in Ancient Mediterranean Society*. Minneapolis: Fortress Press, 2003.

This study offers a comparative study of the organization and practices of churches, synagogues, and associations in the urban life of the Roman Empire.

Hawkins, Cameron. *Roman Artisans and the Urban Economy*. Cambridge: Cambridge University Press, 2016.

Cameron discusses the economic aspects of the imperial artisan economy through an examination of their place in various dimensions of urban life.

Rapp, Claudia, and H. A. Drake, eds. *The City in the Classical and Post-classical World: Changing Contexts of Power and Identity*. Cambridge: Cambridge University Press, 2014.

This collection of essays examines the evolution of ideas about the city and civic practices in the imperial world from the first century to

the start of Byzantium, as well as the role of Christianity in creating
new conceptualizations of urban identity and imagination.
Scheidel, Walter, Ian Morris, and Richard P. Saller, eds. *The
Cambridge Economic History of the Greco-Roman World.*
Cambridge: Cambridge University Press. 2013.
A comprehensive one-volume collection of essays by leading imperial
historians on various aspects of the organization and growth of the
ancient economy from the Bronze Age to late antiquity.

Chapter 5

Joshel, Sandra R. *Slavery in the Roman World.* Cambridge Introduction
to Roman Civilization. New York: Cambridge University
Press, 2013.
Joshel furnishes readers with an introductory overview of the mate-
rial conditions and legal framework of slavery in the western and
eastern empire, with an excellent discussion of slaves in household
and family life, frequently accompanied by images.
Osiek, Carolyn, and David L. Balch, eds. *Families in the New Testament
World: Households and House Churches.* The Family, Religion, and
Culture. Louisville, KY: Westminster John Knox, 1997.
This is a series of essays by leading experts on the material world and
ideological construction of the family in the Roman Empire, with a
view to understanding the role of the household in early Christian
belief and practice.
Osiek, Carolyn, Margaret Y. MacDonald, and Janet H. Tulloch.
A Woman's Place: House Churches in Earliest Christianity.
Minneapolis: Fortress Press, 2006.
Offers a series of chapters dedicated to various aspects of women's lives
and family life in imperial Greek households, with a special focus
on material culture reflected by various New Testament texts.
Rawson, Beryl, ed. *A Companion to Families in the Greek and Roman
Worlds.* Blackwell Companions to the Ancient World. Malden,
MA: Wiley-Blackwell, 2011.
The volume compiles essays by Greek and Roman historians on a
variety of topics relating to family life; it includes discussion of
children, slaves, women, marriage, household religion, domestic
rituals, and so on.

Chapter 6

Foucault, Michel. *The History of Sexuality.* Vol. 3, *The Care of the Self.* Translated by Robert Hurley. New York: Vintage, 1978.
This is a classic work that explores the role of self-examination and regulation of the body and desire in the fashioning of identity in the early Roman Empire.
Martin, Dale B. *The Corinthian Body.* New Haven, CT: Yale University Press, 1999.
Drawing on ancient medical writings, Stoicism, modern anthropological approaches, and feminist and ideological methods of critical analysis, this book examines how ancient ideas of the body and the self played a central role in Corinthian debates.
Remes, Pauliina, and Juha Sihvola, eds. *Ancient Philosophy of the Self.* The New Synthese Historical Library 64. Dordrecht, the Netherlands: Springer, 2010.
This is a collection of essays by various Greek and Roman historians, as well as New Testament scholars, that explores the various ways in which selfhood was approached and conceptualized from the fifth century BCE to the fourteenth century CE. E-book available online at http://www.springer.com/de/book/9781402085956.
Rothschild, Clare K., and Trevor W. Thompson, eds. *Christian Body, Christian Self: Concepts of Early Christian Personhood.* WUNT 284. Tübingen, Germany: Mohr Siebeck, 2011.
The book consists of a series of essays that examine New Testament and contemporary Jewish and extracanonical Christian literature in the light of ancient medical and philosophical theorization of the body and the practices of the self.
Rüpke, Jörg. *The Individual in the Religions of the Ancient Mediterranean.* Oxford: Oxford University Press, 2013.
A collection of essays by leading historians of Greek and Roman religion that contest the notion that the idea of the individual is a modern invention and examine its presence and practices in Greek and Roman religion.

INDEX LOCORUM

SUBJECT INDEX

Page numbers in *italics* indicate illustrations. For specific works and their specific citations, including biblical citations, please consult the **INDEX LOCORUM**.

Paul, the Apostle - movie

Book - "

Shroud of
Turin